Doctrine and Covenants

Expedition

A Study Guide for All Ages

by Paul R. Day

96 97 98 99 00 01 02   10 9 8 7 6 5 4 3 2 1

Doctrine & Covenants Expedition
Cover Illustration by Duane Cude
Covenant Communications, Inc.
ISBN 1-57734-031-0

In this sequel to the Book of Mormon Expedition, it is now ....

    Time for another expedition! Another journey through history!

    To decipher more mysteries. Of latter-day origins. Of God. Of his servants. Of his doctrines and commandments. More treasures, even hidden treasures. Diamonds. Brilliant, of rare colors and lights. Trees. Everlasting, verdant, precious.

    I will again be your guide. This time, with new maps. Follow these maps, keep the Captain's Log, and we will again embark on a journey never to be forgotten!

    Come. The maps beckon. Our forefathers have prepared the way. No toil nor labor shall we fear! We'll find the place which God for us prepared!

                    Your expedition guide,
                    Paul R. Day

Introduction

In this expedition, we will be riding a train into the mountains of the past on a long, curvy track, through tunnels and beautiful scenery. You will have to shovel some coal to keep the engine hot; but you are strong, and there is a luxury car with all the comforts in which you can curl up and enjoy the adventure. You can even bring family members or friends along. When we stop the train, you can find diamonds to put into your pouch, discover rare and precious tree seedlings for transplanting, or dig into the mountain and find other hidden treasures.

This expedition will help you move through the Doctrine and Covenants, section by section, answering the questions in the Captain's Log, noting progress, and collecting various treasures along the way. *Expedition maps* guide you through this journey. The first *map* is the Captain's Log, and is not optional. By completing the Captain's Log, you complete the expedition. In addition, depending on your age, experience, and commitment, you can decide which other maps you will follow and how many treasures you will bring home from your expedition. All maps are achievable; you just have to follow them. Success is dependent not so much on age or experience as on time and determination. The treasures are real. They wait for you.

You may collect six kinds of treasures on this expedition:

1. All that you learn by completing the Captain's Log (pp. 5-57). This includes reading the 138 sections in the Doctrine and Covenants and answering 539 questions. For this endeavor, progress *maps* are provided: a color-in graphic to mark progress (pp. 58-59), milestone divisions with rewards (pp. 60-62), and the milestone record (p. 63).

2. *Diamond* scriptures. These are small, precious gems you collect and mark in your scriptures. There are 32 *diamond* scriptures identified with the ♦ symbol in the Captain's Log. To put these treasures into your pouch and bring them home from your expedition, follow the maps on pages 64-74.

3. *Tree* scriptures. These are larger than *diamonds*, and require more work to bring home and plant. There are 29 *tree* scriptures identified with the 🌲 symbol in the Captain's Log. To put these into your train car and bring them safely out of the mountains, follow the maps on pages 75-86.

4. Mountain *stones*. These are not individual scriptures, but summaries of the more important sections of the Doctrine and Covenants. After you excavate an important section, bringing out *diamonds, trees,* and other treasures, you will want a *stone* to signify the mountain from which you extracted your wealth, and to remember its snow-covered peaks and beautiful valleys. There are 14 large

mountains and 30 small *mountains* identified in the Captain's Log with the Δ and ▲ symbols or *stones*. To safely pack these *stones* into your train car, follow the maps on pages 87-91.

5. *Hidden treasures*. As you complete the Captain's Log and answer the questions, and as you work through the other maps, the Spirit will guide you to hidden groves, valleys of peace, trails of wisdom, and great treasures of knowledge, even hidden treasures (D&C 89:19). Cherish these. Pack them away in your luxury car. Tag them and identify them with markings, even hidden markings. To pack these treasures away, follow the maps on pages 92-93.

6. Journal entries and side-expedition treasures. This is an open-ended map that will extend beyond the confines of the above maps. To pack these treasures away, follow the maps on pages 95-98.

By following these maps, you will come home with a rare collection of treasures. You will establish credentials to become a seasoned explorer, becoming better prepared for more expeditions, and even to become a guide yourself.

I encourage you to follow each map first for yourself. In addition, if you have children on the expedition, help them with their maps. You are their guide. Take pride as their treasures are collected, and help them excavate the *diamonds, trees, mountain stones* and *hidden treasures*. Display the *color-in graphics* in a prominent place. Plan with your children the rewards in the *milestones and rewards* map; and for the final milestone, commit to a crowning reward, a gift of value, that will be a symbol of your love throughout their lives.

As a teacher, you may be more creative in using these maps beyond the directions given. For example, you could use selections from the Captain's Log in a classroom or family home evening activity; you could hand out colored pencils to mark treasures and the color-in graphics; or you could design games to review the memorizations. In this you will be "accounted as the salt of the earth and the savor of men" (D&C 101:39), and be "endowed with power, that ye may give even as I [the Lord] have spoken" (D&C 43:16).

PRD

Expedition Maps

Captain's Log (pages 5-57)

The goal of this expedition is to turn your study of the Doctrine and Covenants into a trek through history, to find treasures along the way, to catalogue and preserve, and to bring the treasures home from the *mountains* of these unique scriptures. The Captain's Log is central. Think of it as a journal of your daytime exploits. Then, after a day's journey, retreat to your luxury car and consider the entries in your journal. Bring out your other expedition maps, note progress, consider where you have traveled, and preserve the treasures you have found.

There are two parts to each question in the Captain's Log. First, the answer. Second, the reference or verse number where the answer is found. Both must be entered to complete a question. In addition, when you come upon a *diamond* scripture (♦), a *tree* scripture (♣), or a mountain *stone* (Δ and ▲) in the Captain's Log, you may want to pause and collect the treasure. Refer to *Collecting diamonds*, *Planting trees*, and *Collecting mountain stones* on pages 64, 75, and 87.

A day's journey may consist of one section, two sections, or if a section is long, just part of a section. The Captain's Log can help you pace your way through these uneven sections. You may simply do a certain number of questions on each leg of your journey, irrespective of the sections they traverse.

Think of each question in the Captain's Log as a pick and shovel into the mountain where the train is stopped. Read the section carefully to find each answer, then record in the log while pondering the significance of your find. As you move from question to question, do not miss the hidden treasures in the words in focus, sent from above. These may come while basking in the shade of a mountain, perhaps with shovel in hand, or maybe while resting in your luxury car as you record the events of the day. Preserve the hidden treasures by highlighting impressive passages with colored pencils, or entering in the *hidden treasures* table (p. 92), or writing in your personal journal (p. 95).

Of course the questions in the Captain's Log cannot touch upon all the verses. There are many "diamonds in the rough," so to speak, between the excavations. But the questions do focus on significant words, and each missing word should draw you to the heart of a special message. Therefore, ponder the whisperings of the Spirit, and the hidden treasures will come, and great shall be your reward. Do not always rush to the next question. If you slow down and savor the words, if your peer into the *diamonds*, plant the *trees*, and collect *hidden treasures*, the doctrines of the gospel will flow into your mind and heart.

In the Book of Mormon expedition, you were to read each chapter first, before going to the questions for that chapter. In this expedition, however, the flow is different. There is little or no story line, and your primary purpose is to study the text, find scriptures worth saving, and learn their context. Some sections are so long and full that they cannot be casually read, while other sections are only a verse or two long. Therefore, tackle them any way you want, even out of order sometimes. Just be sure to find the treasures hiding there in the rocks and bushes!

Finally, as you travel through the scriptures, verse by verse, remember that although in their historical context many of the sections were targeted to specific individuals, we should receive these scriptures as the Lord speaking to us individually and in our time. The Lord declares in his preface that his voice is unto *all* men (D&C 1:2), and that we should search these commandments (D&C 1:37). Section 4 is to "ye that embark in the service of God" (D&C 4:2), and Section 11 is unto "all who have good desires" (D&C 11:27). And so it is with all the revelations. When the Lord tells Joseph he should not have feared man more than God (D&C 3:11), when he tells Hyrum to first obtain his word before seeking to declare it (D&C 11:21), when he speaks to Emma Smith (D&C 25:1,16), he speaks to all of us. "What I say unto one I say unto all" (D&C 61:36).

Following the Captain's Log are the other *maps*. Turn now to page 58 and examine these maps before you begin your expedition.

Captain's Log

Section 1:   Δ

1. From the heading: "This section constitutes the Lord's _____ to the doctrines, covenants, and commandments given in this dispensation."

2. "For verily the voice of the Lord is unto all men, and there is none to _____ . " D&C 1:____

3. "And the voice of warning shall be unto all people, by the mouths of my _____ , whom I have chosen in these last days." D&C 1:____

4. "Unto the day when the Lord shall come to _____ unto every man according to his work, and _____ to every man according to the measure which he has measured to his fellow man." D&C 1:____

5. The Lord, knowing the calamity which should come, called upon his servant Joseph Smith, Jun., " and spake unto him from heaven, and gave him _____ ." D&C 1:____

6. "The _____ things of the world shall come forth and break down the mighty and strong ones." D&C 1:____

7. God gave these commandments unto his servants in their weakness, after the manner of their _____ , that they might come to understanding. D&C 1:____

8. "And inasmuch as they were _____ they might be made strong, and blessed from on high, and receive knowledge from time to time." D&C 1:____

9. "For I the Lord cannot look upon _____ with the least degree of allowance." D&C 1:____ ✦

10. "And he that repents not, from him shall be taken even the _____ which he has received; for my Spirit shall not always strive with man." D&C 1:____

11. "_____ these commandments, for they are true and faithful, and the prophecies and promises which are in them shall all be fulfilled." D&C 1:____

12. Does God excuse himself? _____ Will his word pass away? _____ Is it the same whether by his own voice or by the voice of his servants? _____ D&C 1:___

Section 2:

13. From the heading: This section is an extract from the words of _____
_____ .

14. "Behold, I will reveal unto you the _____ , by the hand of Elijah the prophet." D&C 2:____

15. "And he shall plant in the hearts of the children the _____ made to the fathers." D&C 2:____

Section 3:   ▲

16. From the heading: This section relates to the loss of 116 pages of manuscript translated from the first part of the Book of Mormon, which was called the "Book of _____ ."

17. Can the works and designs and purposes of God be frustrated? _____
D&C 3:____

18. "For God doth not walk in _____ paths, neither doth he turn to the right hand nor to the left." D&C 3:____ ✦

19. The Lord told Joseph, "For, behold, you should not have _____ man more than God." D&C 3:____ ✦

20. The Lord told Joseph that because of transgression he could fall, but if he would repent he would again be called to the work. "Except thou do this, thou shalt be delivered up and become as other men, and have no more _____ ."
D&C 3:____

21. Joseph lost his privileges for a season, "For thou hast suffered the counsel of thy _____ to be trampled upon from the beginning." D&C 3:____

Section 4:   ▲

22. From the heading: This revelation was given through Joseph Smith to
_____ .

23. "Therefore, O ye that embark in the service of God, see that ye serve him with all your _____ , _____ , _____ and _____ ." D&C 4:____

24. "And _____ , _____ , _____ and _____ , with an eye single to the glory of God, qualify him for the work." D&C 4:____

Section 5: ▲

25. From the heading: This revelation was given through Joseph Smith at the request of _____ _____ .

26. Martin Harris desired a witness that Joseph Smith had the plates. However, Joseph had entered a covenant with the Lord not to show them except to those commanded him. The Lord said, "Behold, if they will not believe _____ words, they would not believe you, my servant Joseph, if it were possible that you should show them _____ these things which I have committed unto you." D&C 5:____

27. The Lord said that in addition to Joseph's testimony there would be the testimony of _____ servants, to be called, ordained, and shown these things. D&C 5:____

28. Of these three servants, "Yea, they shall know of a surety that these things are true, for from _____ will I declare it unto them." D&C 5:____

29. "I will give them _____ that they may behold and view these things as they are." D&C 5:____

30. The church will rise up and come forth "... out of the wilderness--clear as the _____ , and fair as the _____ , and terrible as an _____ with banners." D&C 5:____

31. Did the Lord promise the man [Martin Harris] who desired the witness, that he would be granted to view the things he desired to see if he would bow down and humble himself in mighty prayer and faith, and in the sincerity of his heart? _____ D&C 5:____

32. The Lord said to Joseph, "Yea, for this cause I have said: Stop, and _____ _____ until I command thee, and I will provide means whereby thou mayest accomplish the thing which I have commanded thee." D&C 5:____

Section 6: ▲

33. From the heading: This revelation was given to Joseph Smith and _____ _____ , who began his labors as scribe in the translation of the Book of Mormon and had already received a divine manifestation.

34. The word of God is _____ and _____, sharper than a two-edged sword. D&C 6:____

35. "Seek not for riches but for _____ , and behold, the mysteries of God shall be unfolded unto you, and then shall you be made rich. Behold, he that hath _____ _____ is rich." D&C 6:____ ♣

36. "Verily, verily, I say unto you, even as you _____ of me so it shall be unto you; and if you _____ , you shall be the means of doing much good in this generation."   D&C 6:____

37. "Behold thou hast a _____ , and blessed art thou because of thy _____ . Remember it is sacred and cometh from above."   D&C 6:____

38. "Make not thy gift known unto any save it by those who are of thy faith. _____ not with sacred things."   D&C 6:____   ✦

39. "Behold, thou knowest that thou hast inquired of me and I did _____ thy mind; and now I tell thee these things that thou mayest know that thou hast been _____ by the Spirit of truth."   D&C 6:____

40. Is there anyone besides God who knows the thoughts and intents of your heart? _____   D&C 6:____

41. "Did I not speak _____ to your mind concerning the matter? What greater witness can you have than from God?   D&C 6:____   ✦

42. "Fear not to do _____ , my sons, for whatsoever ye sow, that shall ye also reap."   D&C 6:____

43. "_____ unto me in every thought; doubt not, fear not."   D&C 6:____   ✦

Section 7:   ▲

44. From the heading: This revelation is "a translated version of the record made on parchment by _____ and hidden up by himself."

45. John was told that whatsoever he desired, it would be granted unto him. He said, "Lord, give unto me power over _____ , that I may live and bring souls unto thee."   D&C 7:____

46. Peter was also granted a wish. His desire was that he might "... speedily come unto me in my _____ ."   D&C 7:____

47. John had undertaken a greater work. "... therefore I will make him as _____ fire and a _____ angel; he shall minister for those who shall be heirs of salvation who dwell on the earth."   D&C 7:____

Section 8:   ▲

48. From the heading: This section has to do with Oliver Cowdery's desire to be endowed with the gift of _____ .

49. "Yea, behold, I will tell you in your _____ and in your _____ , by the Holy Ghost, which shall come upon you and which shall dwell in your heart." D&C 8:____ ♣

50. "Remember that without _____ you can do nothing; therefore ask in faith. Trifle not with these things; do not ask for that which you ought not." D&C 8:___

Section 9: ▲

51. From the heading: Oliver Cowdery is admonished to be patient, and is urged to be content to write, rather than to attempt to _____ .

52. "Behold, you have not understood; you have supposed that I would give it unto you, when you took no _____ save it was to _____ me." D&C 9:___

53. "But, behold, I say unto you, that you must study it out in your _____ ; then you must ask me if it be right, and if it is right I will cause that your bosom shall burn within you; therefore, you shall _____ that it is right." D&C 9:____ ♣

54. "But if it be not right you shall have no such feelings, but you shall have a _____ of thought that shall cause you to forget the thing which is wrong." D&C 9:____

Section 10: ▲

55. This section is out of chronological order. It belongs after section ____ because it was received at that time, and has to do with the same events (lost 116 pages). Refer to the "Chronological Order of Contents" just before section 1.

56. Because Joseph had delivered up the writings into the hands of a wicked man, the Lord said to him, "And you also lost your gift at the same time, and your mind became _____ ." D&C 10:____

57. "Do not run faster or labor more than you have _____ and _____ provided." D&C 10:____ ◆

58. "And their hearts are corrupt, and full of wickedness and abominations; and they love darkness rather than light, because their _____ are _____ ; therefore they will not ask of me." D&C 10:___

59. "Verily, verily, I say unto you, wo be unto him that lieth to _____ because he supposeth that another lieth to _____ , for such are not exempt from the justice of God." D&C 10:____

9

60. The Lord told Joseph to translate the plates of Nephi to cover the same time period as the translation that was lost, down to the reign of king Benjamin. He explained, "Behold, there are many things engraven upon the plates of Nephi which do throw greater views upon my _____ ; therefore, it is wisdom in me that you should translate this first part of the engravings of Nephi."

61. "And this I do that I may establish my gospel, that there may not be so much _____ ; yea, Satan doth stir up the hearts of the people to _____ concerning the points of my doctrine." D&C 10:____

Section 11:   ▲

62. From the heading: This revelation was given through Joseph Smith to
_____ .

63. "Behold, the field is white already to harvest; therefore, whoso _____ to reap let him thrust in his sickle with his might." D&C 11:____

64. "Behold, thou hast a _____ , or thou shalt have a _____ if thou wilt desire of me in faith, with an honest heart, believing in the power of Jesus Christ, or in my power which speaketh unto thee." D&C 11:____

65. "Verily, verily, I say unto you, I will impart unto you of my Spirit, which shall enlighten your _____ , which shall fill your _____ with joy." D&C 11:____

66. "Seek not to declare my word, but first seek to _____ my word, and then shall your tongue be loosed; then, if you desire, you shall have my _____ and my _____ , yea, the power of God unto the convincing of men."
D&C 11:____ ♣

67. "Deny not the spirit of _____ , nor the spirit of _____ , for wo unto him that denieth these things." D&C 11:____

68. The Lord clarifies that this revelation is not just for Hyrum. "Behold, I speak unto _____ who have good desires, and have thrust in their sickle to reap."
D&C 11:____

Section 12:

69. From the heading: This revelation was given through Joseph Smith to
_____ .

70. "And no one can assist in this work except he shall be humble and full of love, having faith, hope, and charity, being _____ in all things, whatsoever shall be entrusted to his care." D&C 12:____

Section 13:

71. From the heading: The ordination of Joseph Smith and Oliver Cowdery to the Aaronic Priesthood was done by the hands of an angel, "... the same that is called _____ _____ _____ in the New Testament."

72. "Upon you my fellow servants, in the name of _____ I confer the Priesthood of Aaron, which holds the keys of the _____ of angels, and of the gospel of _____ , and of baptism by immersion for the _____ of sins."   D&C 13:____

Section 14:

73. From the heading: At whose home did the Prophet establish his residence until the work of translation was carried to completion? _____

74. "And, if you keep my commandments and endure to the end you shall have _____ _____ , which gift is the greatest of all the gifts of God." D&C 14:____

Section 15:

75. From the heading: John Whitmer later became one of the _____ Witnesses.

76. The Lord told John Whitmer that the thing which would be of the most worth unto him would be to declare _____ unto this people.   D&C 15:____

Section 16:

77. From the heading: This revelation was given through Joseph Smith to

_____ .

78. Was Peter's desire the same as his brother John's in section 15? _____ D&C 16:____

Section 17:

79. From the heading: This revelation was given through the Urim and Thummim to _____ special witnesses.

80. "Behold, I say unto you, that you must rely upon my word, which if you do with full purpose of heart, you shall have a view of the _____ , and also of the _____ , the _____ of Laban, the _____ _____ _____ , which were given to the brother of Jared upon the mount, when he talked with the Lord face to face, and the miraculous _____ which were given to Lehi while in the wilderness, on the borders of the Red Sea."   D&C 17:____

81. Did these witnesses receive the same power, the same faith, and the same gift like unto Joseph Smith? _____   D&C 17:____

Section 18:

82. From the heading: This revelation was given in response to supplication for knowledge on the matter of the _____ Priesthood.

83. "Remember the worth of _____ is great in the sight of God."   D&C 18:____ ✦

84. "And if it so be that you should labor all your days in crying repentance unto this people, and bring, save it be _____ _____ unto me, how great shall be your joy with him in the kingdom of my Father!"   D&C 18:____

85. "Take upon you the name of Christ, and speak the truth in _____ ."   D&C 18:____

86. "And by their _____ and their works you shall know them."   D&C 18:____

Section 19:   ▲

87. From the heading: Joseph introduced this as "a commandment of God and not of man, to Martin Harris, given by him who is _____ ."

88. Did Christ retain all power, even to the destroying of Satan? _____   D&C 19:___

89. "For, behold, the mystery of godliness, how great is it! For, behold, I am _____ , and the punishment which is given from my hand is _____ punishment, for _____ is my name."   D&C 19:____

90. "For behold, I, God, have suffered these things for all, that they might not _____ if they would repent."   D&C 19:____ 🌲

91. "And thou shalt declare _____ tidings, yea, publish it upon the mountains, and upon every _____ place."   D&C 19:____

92. "And of _____ thou shalt not talk, but thou shalt declare repentance and faith on the Savior."   D&C 19:____

Section 20:   Δ

93. From the heading: This is a revelation on Church Organization and

_____ .

94. "And gave unto him _____ which inspired him."   D&C 20:____ ✦

95. "And we know that justification through the _____ of our Lord and Savior
    Jesus Christ is just and true."   D&C 20:____

96. Must those who are baptized have a determination to serve Jesus Christ to the
    end? _____   D&C 20:____

97. Who are to conduct the meetings as they are led by the Holy Ghost? _____
    _____   D&C 20:____

98. After the duties of the elders, priests, teachers, and members, the manner of
    administering baptism is given: "The person who is called of God and has
    _____ from Jesus Christ to baptize, shall go down into the water
    with the person who has presented himself or herself for baptism." The
    baptismal prayer is then given.   D&C 20:____

99. The sacramental prayers are next given. In verse 79, footnote "a" cross
    references to the scripture that explains why water was later substituted for
    wine. What scripture is given in footnote *79a*? _____

Section 21:

100. From the heading: This revelation was given at the organization of the _____
     in the home of Peter Whitmer, Sen.

101. On what date was the Church organized? _____   D&C 21:____

102. "For by doing these things the gates of hell shall not prevail against you; yea,
     and the Lord God will _____ the powers of darkness from before
     you, and cause the heavens to _____ for your good, and his name's glory."
     D&C 21:____

Section 22:

103. From the heading: This revelation was given because some who had previously
     been baptized desired to unite with the Church without _____ .

104. "Wherefore, enter ye in at the gate, as I have commanded, and seek not to
     _____ your God. Amen."   D&C 22:____

Section 23:

105. From the heading: This revelation was given as the result of the earnest desire on the part of the five persons named to know of their respective _____ .

106. Hyrum was told he was under no condemnation, "and thy heart is opened, and thy tongue loosed; and thy calling is to exhortation, and to _____ the church continually."   D&C 23:____

Section 24:

107. From the heading: Given to Joseph Smith and Oliver Cowdery. Because persecution had become intense, these revelations were given at this time to strengthen, _____ , and instruct them.

108. "Be patient in _____ , for thou shalt have many; but endure them, for, lo, I am with thee, even unto the end of thy days."   D&C 24:____

109. "And in temporal labors thou shalt not have _____ , for this is not thy calling. Attend to thy calling and thou shalt have wherewith to magnify thine office, and to expound all _____ ."   D&C 24:____

Section 25:   Δ

110. "Hearken unto the voice of the Lord your God, while I speak unto you, _____ _____ , my daughter; for verily I say unto you, all those who receive my gospel are sons and daughters in my kingdom."   D&C 25:____

111. "Behold, thy sins are forgiven thee, and thou art an _____ lady, whom I have called."   D&C 25:____

112. " _____ not because of the things which thou hast not seen, for they are withheld from thee and from the world."   D&C 25:____

113. "And the office of thy calling shall be for a _____ unto my servant, Joseph Smith, Jun., thy husband, in his afflictions, with _____ words, in the spirit of meekness."   D&C 25:____

114. Was Emma to be a scribe for her husband? _____   D&C 25:____

115. "And thou shalt be ordained under his hand to expound _____ , and to _____ the church, according as it shall be given thee by my Spirit.   D&C 25:____

116. "And it shall be given thee, also, to make a selection of sacred _____ , as it shall be given thee, which is pleasing unto me, to be had in my church."
D&C 25:____

117. "For my soul delighteth in the song of the _____ ; yea, the song of the righteous is a _____ unto me, and it shall be answered with a blessing upon their heads." D&C 25:____ ◆

Section 26:

118. "And all things shall be done by _____ consent in the church, by much prayer and faith, for all things you shall receive by _____ ." D&C 26:____

Section 27:

119. From the heading: When Joseph set out to procure wine for the sacrament, he was met by a _____ _____ and received this revelation.

120. "For, behold, I say unto you, that it mattereth not what ye shall eat or what ye shall drink when ye partake of the _____ , if it so be that ye do it with an eye _____ to my glory." D&C 27:____

121. "Wherefore, lift up your hearts and _____ , and gird up your loins, and take upon you my _____ _____ , that ye may be able to withstand the evil day, having done all, that ye may be able to stand." D&C 27:____

Section 28:

122. From the heading: This revelation was directed to Oliver Cowdery, who was wrongly influenced by Hiram Page, who professed to be receiving revelation by the aid of a _____ .

123. "But thou shalt not write by way of commandment, but by _____ ."
D&C 28:____

124. "And thou shalt not command him who is at thy _____ , and at the _____ of the church." D&C 28:____

125. "For I have given him the keys of the _____ , and the revelations which are sealed, until I shall appoint unto them another in his stead." D&C 28:____

Section 29: ▲

126. From the heading: This revelation was given in the presence of _____ elders.
127. "Lift up your hearts and be glad, for I am in your midst, and am your
     _____ with the Father."   D&C 29:____
128. Who will stand at the right hand of Jesus on the day of his coming in a pillar of
     fire, clothed with robes of righteousness, and crowns upon their heads?
     _____ D&C 29:____
129. What shall sound both long and loud when the earth shall quake and the dead
     shall come forth? _____   D&C 29:____
130. Will men again begin to deny their God at the end of the thousand years? ____
     D&C 29:____
131. "For all old things shall pass away, and all things shall become new, even the
     _____ and the _____ ."   D&C 29:____
132. "Wherefore, verily I say unto you that all things unto me are _____ ,
     and not at any time have I given unto you a law which was _____ ."
     D&C 29:____ ♣
133. Speaking of little children, "Wherefore, they cannot sin, for _____ is not
     given unto Satan to tempt little children, until they begin to become
     _____ before me."   D&C 29:____

Section 30:

134. From the heading: This revelation was given to David, Peter, and John
     _____ .
135. "But your _____ has been on the things of the earth more than on the things
     of me, your Maker, and the _____ whereunto you have been called."
     D&C 30:____

Section 31:

136. From the heading: This revelation was given to _____ .
137. "Lift up your heart and rejoice, for the hour of your _____ is come; and
     your tongue shall be loosed, and you shall declare glad tidings of great joy unto
     this generation."   D&C 31:____
138. "Be patient in afflictions, _____ not against those that _____ ."
     D&C 31:____

Section 32:

139. From the heading: This revelation has to do with whether elders should be sent to _____ .

140. "And they shall give heed to that which is _____ , and pretend to no other revelation; and they shall pray always that I may unfold the same to their understanding." D&C 32:____

Section 33:

141. "Open your mouths and they shall be _____ , and you shall become even as _____ of old, who journeyed from Jerusalem in the wilderness." D&C 33:____

142. "And the Book of Mormon and the _____ _____ are given of me for your instruction; and the power of my Spirit _____ all things." D&C 33:____

Section 34:

143. Orson Pratt was called, "To lift up your voice as with the sound of a _____ , both long and loud." D&C 34:____

Section 35:

144. From the heading: This revelation was given to Joseph Smith and Sidney Rigdon. Rigdon was called by divine appointment to serve as the Prophet's _____ .

145. "For I am God, and mine arm is not shortened; and I will show _____ , _____ , and _____ , unto all those who believe on my name." D&C 35:____

146. "Wherefore, I call upon the weak things of the world, those who are _____ and _____ , to thrash the nations by the power of my Spirit." D&C 35:____

147. "Keep all the commandments and covenants by which ye are bound; and I will cause the heavens to shake for your _____ , and Satan shall tremble and Zion shall rejoice upon the hills and _____ ." D&C 35:____

Section 36:

148. The Lord said to Edward Partridge, "And I will lay my _____ upon you by the hand of my servant Sidney Rigdon, and you shall receive my Spirit, the Holy Ghost, even the Comforter, which shall teach you the _____ things of the kingdom."   D&C 36:____

Section 37:

149. The Saints are called to gather at the Ohio. "Behold, I say unto you that it is not expedient in me that ye should translate any more until ye shall go to the Ohio, and this because of the _____ and for your _____ ."   D&C 37:____

Section 38:

150. "Thus saith the Lord your God, even Jesus Christ, the Great I Am, Alpha and Omega, the _____ and the _____ ."   D&C 38:____
151. "But behold, the residue of the wicked have I kept in chains of _____ until the judgment of the great day."   D&C 38:____
152. "But behold, verily, verily, I say unto you that mine eyes are upon you. I am in your _____ and ye cannot _____ me."   D&C 38:____
153. "And I have made the earth _____ , and behold it is my footstool, wherefore, again I will stand upon it."   D&C 38:____
154. "Wherefore, hear my voice and follow me, and you shall be a free people, and ye shall have no laws but my laws when I come, for I am your _____ , and what can stay my hand?"   D&C 38:____
155. "Behold, this I have given unto you as a parable, and it is even as I am. I say unto you, be _____ ; and if ye are not _____ ye are not mine."   D&C 38:___
156. "I tell you these things because of your prayers; wherefore, treasure up _____ in your bosoms, lest the wickedness of men reveal these things unto you by their wickedness, in a manner which shall speak in your ears with a voice louder than that which shall shake the earth; but if ye are _____ ye shall not fear."   D&C 38:____ ✦

Section 39:

157. "And verily, verily, I say unto you, he that receiveth my _____ receiveth me; and he that receiveth not my _____ receiveth not me." D&C 39:____

158. "But, behold, the days of thy _____ are come, if thou wilt hearken to my voice, which saith unto thee: _____ and be baptized, and wash away your sins, calling on my name, and you shall receive my Spirit, and a blessing so great as you never have known." D&C 39:____

Section 40:

159. "And he received the word with gladness, but straightway Satan tempted him; and the fear of _____ and the cares of the world caused him to reject the word." D&C 40:____

Section 41:

160. "Hearken, O ye elders of my church whom I have called, behold I give unto you a commandment, that ye shall _____ yourselves together to _____ upon my word." D&C 41:____

161. "These words are given unto you, and they are pure before me; wherefore, beware how you _____ them, for they are to be answered upon your souls in the day of judgment." D&C 41:____

Section 42:   Δ

162. From the heading: The Prophet specifies this revelation as "embracing the _____ of the Church."

163. "And ye shall go forth in the power of my Spirit, preaching my gospel, two by two, in my name, lifting up your voices as with the sound of a trump, declaring my word like unto _____ of God." D&C 42:____

164. "And the Spirit shall be given unto you by the prayer of faith; and if ye receive not the Spirit ye shall not _____ ." D&C 42:____ ✦

165. "Thou shalt not speak evil of thy _____ , nor do him any harm." D&C 42:____

166. "Thou shalt not be _____ ; for he that is _____ shall not eat the bread nor wear the garments of the laborer." D&C 42:____

167. "And it shall come to pass that those that die in me shall not taste of death, for it shall be _____ unto them." D&C 42:____

168. "If thou shalt ask, thou shalt receive _____ upon _____ , _____ upon _____ , that thou mayest know the mysteries and peaceable things---that which bringeth joy, that which bringeth life eternal." D&C 42:____

Section 43:

169. Some people were making false claims as revelators (heading). But commandments and revelations are to come only through the one appointed. If the one having this gift has it taken from him, will he have power to appoint another in his stead? _____ D&C 43:____

170. "And now, behold, I give unto you a commandment, that when ye are assembled together ye shall _____ and _____ each other." D&C 43:____

171. "Again I say, hearken ye elders of my church, whom I have appointed: Ye are not sent forth to be _____ , but to _____ the children of men the things which I have put into your hands by the power of my Spirit." D&C 43:____ ♠

172. "And ye are to be taught from ____ _____ . Sanctify yourselves and ye shall be endowed with _____ , that ye may give even as I have spoken." D&C 43:____

173. "Hearken ye to these words. Behold, I am Jesus Christ, the Savior of the world. _____ these things up in your hearts, and let the solemnities of eternity rest upon your minds." D&C 43:____

Section 44:

174. "Behold, I say unto you, that ye must visit the _____ and the _____ and administer to their relief." D&C 44:____

175. The Lord spoke of Enoch and his brethren who were separated from the earth. Then he introduced the theme of this revelation by recalling what he said to his disciples as he stood before them in the flesh, "As ye have asked of me concerning the _____ of my coming, in the day when I shall come in my _____ in the clouds of heaven." D&C 45:____

176. "And when the times of the Gentiles is come in, a light shall break forth among them that sit in darkness, and it shall be the _____ of my _____ ." D&C 45:____

177. "But my disciples shall stand in _____ places, and shall not be _____ ." D&C 45:____

178. "And it shall come to pass that he that feareth me shall be _____ _____ for the great day of the Lord to come, even for the signs of the coming of the Son of Man." D&C 45:____

179. "And calamity shall cover the mocker, and the scorner shall be consumed: and they that have _____ for _____ shall be hewn down and cast into the fire." D&C 45:____

180. "For they that are wise and have received the truth, and have taken the Holy Spirit for their _____ , and have not been _____ ---verily I say unto you, they shall not be hewn down and cast into the fire, but shall abide the day." D&C 45:____

181. Did the Lord tell the Prophet that he should now translate the New Testament? _____ D&C 45:____

182. "And it shall be called the New Jerusalem, a land of _____ , a city of _____ , a place of _____ for the saints of the Most High God." D&C 45:____

Section 46:   ▲

183. "But ye are commanded in all things to ask of God, who giveth _____ ; and that which the Spirit testifies unto you even so I would that ye should do in all holiness of heart, walking uprightly before me, _____ the end of your salvation." D&C 46:____

184. "Wherefore, beware lest ye are deceived; and that ye may not be deceived seek ye earnestly the _____ _____ , always remembering for what they are given." D&C 46:____ ✦

185. "For all have not every _____ given unto them; for there are many _____ ,
and to every man is given a _____ by the Spirit of God." D&C 46:___
186. "And all these gifts come from God, for the _____ of the children of
God." D&C 46:___

Section 47:

187. "Wherefore, it shall be given him, inasmuch as he is faithful, by the Comforter, to
_____ these things." D&C 47:___

Section 48:

188. "It must needs be necessary that ye save all the _____ that ye can, and
that ye obtain all that ye can in righteousness, that in time ye may be enabled to
purchase land for an inheritance, even the city." D&C 48:___

Section 49:

189. "Behold, I say unto you, that they desire to know the truth in part, but not ____ ,
for they are not right before me and must needs repent." D&C 49:___
190. Do the angels in heaven know the hour and the day of the coming of the Son?
_____ D&C 49:___
191. "And again, verily I say unto you, that whoso forbiddeth to _____ is not
ordained of God, for _____ is ordained of God unto man." D&C 49:___
192. "For, behold, the beasts of the field and the fowls of the air, and that which
cometh of the earth, is _____ for the use of man for food and for
raiment, and that he might have in _____ ." D&C 49:___

Section 50:   ▲

193. The Lord asked the question, "Unto what were ye ordained?" His answer: "To
preach my gospel by the Spirit, even the _____ which was sent
forth to teach the _____ ." D&C 50:___
194. "And that which doth not _____ is not of God, and is darkness."
D&C 50:___ ✦

22

195. "That which is of God is _____ ; and he that receiveth _____ , and continueth in God, receiveth more _____ ; and that _____ groweth brighter and brighter until the perfect day."   D&C 50:___

196. "Behold, ye are little children and ye cannot _____ all things now; ye must grow in _____ and in the knowledge of the truth."   D&C 50:___

197. "Wherefore, I am in your midst, and I am the good _____ , and the _____ of Israel. He that buildeth upon this rock shall never fall."   D&C 50:___

Section 51:

198. The Saints began to arrive in Ohio, and arrangements had to be made for their settlement. The Lord said, "And thus I grant unto this people a _____ of organizing themselves according to my laws."   D&C 51:___

199. But they were told they would only have this land for a little season, then they would move on. "And the hour and the day is not given unto them, wherefore let them act upon this land as for _____ , and this shall turn unto them for their good."   D&C 51:___

Section 52:

200. The Lord gave a pattern in all things, that his people might not be deceived, in which he said, "He that speaketh, whose spirit is _____ , whose _____ is meek and edifieth, the same is of God if he obey mine ordinances."   D&C 52:___

201. "And the days have come; according to men's _____ it shall be done unto them."   D&C 52:___

Section 53:

202. "Take upon you mine _____ , even that of an elder, to preach _____ and _____ and _____ of sins, according to my word, and the reception of the Holy Spirit by the laying on of hands."   D&C 53:___

Section 54:

203. "Behold, verily, verily, I say unto you, my servant Newel Knight, you shall stand
_____ in the office whereunto I have appointed you." D&C 54:____

Section 55:

204. W.W. Phelps is called and chosen. "And again, you shall be ordained to assist
my servant Oliver Cowdery to do the work of _____ , and of selecting
and writing _____ for schools in this church, that little children also may
receive _____ before me as is pleasing unto me." D&C 55:___

Section 56:

205. The Lord condemns rich men who will not give to the poor. He condemns poor
men whose hearts are not broken, whose spirits are not contrite, who are
greedy and will not labor with their own hands. But he ends with a blessing on
the poor who are pure in heart, for the fatness of the earth shall be theirs. "And
their generations shall inherit the _____ from generation to generation,
forever and ever." D&C 56:____

Section 57:

206. From the heading: This revelation was given to the Prophet in Missouri as he
contemplated the lack of civilization, refinement, and religion among the people
generally. He exclaimed in yearning prayer, "When will the _____
blossom as the rose? When will Zion be built up in her _____ , and where
will thy _____ stand?"
207. "And thus let those of whom I have spoken be _____ in the land of
Zion, as speedily as can be, with their families, to do those things even as I
have spoken." D&C 57:____

Section 58:   ▲

208. "For after much _____ come the blessings." D&C 58:____ ◆

209. "For behold, it is not meet that I should _____ in all things; for he that is _____ in all things, the same is a slothful and not a wise servant; wherefore he receiveth no reward." D&C 58:____ ♣

210. "Verily I say, men should be _____ engaged in a good cause, and do many things of their own _____ _____ , and bring to pass much righteousness." D&C 58:____ ♣

211. "For the _____ is in them, wherein they are _____ unto themselves. And inasmuch as men do good they shall in nowise lose their reward." D&C 58:____

212. "Behold, he who has repented of his sins, the same is forgiven, and I, the Lord, _____ them no more." D&C 58:____ ◆

213. "By this ye may know if a man repenteth of his sins---behold, he will confess them and _____ them." D&C 58:____

Section 59:   ▲

214. "Thou shalt love thy neighbor as thyself. Thou shalt not steal; neither commit adultery, nor kill, nor do anything _____ _____ ____ ." D&C 59:____

215. "For verily this is a day appointed unto you to rest from your labors, and to pay thy _____ unto the Most High." D&C 59:____

216. "And on this day thou shalt do none other thing, only let thy food be prepared with _____ of heart that thy fasting may be perfect, or, in other words, that thy _____ may be full." D&C 59:____

217. "Yea, all things which come of the earth, in the season thereof, are made for the _____ and the use of man, both to _____ the eye and to _____ the heart." D&C 59:____

218. "And in nothing doth man _____ God, or against none is his wrath kindled, save those who _____ not his hand in all things, and obey not his commandments." D&C 59:____

219. "But learn that he who doeth the works of righteousness shall receive his reward, even _____ in this world, and eternal life in the world to come." D&C 59:____

Section 60:

220. "But with some I am not well pleased, for they will not open their _____ , but they hide the talent which I have given unto them, because of the _____ of man. Wo unto such, for mine anger is kindled against them." D&C 60:___

221. "For I, the Lord, rule in the heavens above, and among the armies of the earth; and in the day when I shall make up my _____ , all men shall know what it is that bespeaketh the power of God." D&C 60:___

222. Did the Lord say, "it mattereth not unto me," concerning some choices the elders were to make? _____ D&C 60:___

Section 61:

223. From the heading: "Elder William W. Phelps, in daylight vision, saw the _____ riding in power upon the face of the waters."

224. "But verily I say unto you, that it is not needful for this whole company of mine elders to be moving _____ upon the waters, whilst the inhabitants on either side are perishing in unbelief." D&C 61:___

225. By whose mouth did the Lord curse the waters in the last days? _____ D&C 61:___

226. "And now, verily I say unto you, and what I say unto _____ I say unto _____ , be of good cheer, little children; for I am in your midst, and I have not forsaken you." D&C 61:___

Section 62:

227. "Behold, and hearken, O ye elders of my church, saith the Lord your God, even Jesus Christ, your advocate, who knoweth the _____ of man and how to _____ them who are tempted." D&C 62:___

228. "Nevertheless, ye are blessed, for the testimony which ye have borne is _____ in heaven for the angels to look upon; and they _____ over you, and your sins are forgiven you." D&C 62:___

229. Similar to section 60, the Lord tells the elders to do what seems good to them. He is willing to let them decide. "These things remain with you to do according to _____ and the _____ of the Spirit." D&C 62:___

Section 63:

230. "Wherefore, I, the Lord, am not pleased with those among you who have sought after _____ and _____ for faith, and not for the good of men unto my glory."   D&C 63:___

231. "But unto him that keepeth my commandments I will give the _____ of my kingdom, and the same shall be in him a well of _____ water, springing up unto everlasting life."   D&C 63:___

232. "Yea, and blessed are the dead that die in the Lord, from henceforth, when the Lord shall come, and _____ things shall pass away, and all things become _____ , they shall rise from the dead and shall not die after, and shall receive an inheritance before the Lord, in the holy city."   D&C 63:___

233. After the Lord comes (in the millennium), will children grow up until they become old? _____   D&C 63:___

234. "Remember that that which cometh from above is _____ , and must be spoken with care, and by _____ of the Spirit; and in this there is no condemnation, and ye receive the Spirit through prayer."   D&C 63:___

Section 64:

235. "My disciples, in days of old, sought occasion against one another and forgave not one another in their _____; and for this evil they were _____ and sorely chastened."   D&C 64:___

236. "I, the Lord, will forgive whom I will forgive, but of you it is _____ to forgive _____ men."   D&C 64:___

237. "Behold, now it is called today until the coming of the Son of Man, and verily it is a day of _____ , and a day for the tithing of my people: for he that is tithed shall not be _____ at his coming."   D&C 64:___

238. "Wherefore, be not _____ in well-doing, for ye are laying the foundation of a great work. And out of _____ things proceedeth that which is great."
D&C 64:___ ♣

239. "Behold, the Lord requireth the _____ and a _____ mind; and the willing and obedient shall eat the good of the land of Zion in these last days."
D&C 64:___ ♣

Section 65:

240. "Pray unto the Lord, call upon his holy name, make known his _____
works among the people." D&C 65:____

241. Two kingdoms are mentioned. The Son of Man shall come clothed in the
brightness of his glory to meet the kingdom of _____ which is set up on the
earth. D&C 65:____

242. "Wherefore, may the kingdom of God go forth, that the kingdom of _____
may come." D&C 65:____

Section 66:

243. "Seek not to be _____ . Forsake all unrighteousness." D&C 66:___

244. "Keep these sayings, for they are true and faithful; and thou shalt _____
thine office, and push many people to Zion with songs of _____
joy upon their heads." D&C 66:____

Section 67:

245. "Ye endeavored to believe that ye should receive the blessing which was offered
unto you; but behold, verily I say unto you there were _____ in your hearts,
and verily this is the reason that ye did not _____ ." D&C 67:____

246. Speaking of the revelations received to this point: "For ye know that there is no
unrighteousness in them, and that which is righteous cometh down from
_____ , from the Father of _____ ." D&C 67:____

247. "For no man has seen God at any time in the flesh, except _____ by
the Spirit of God." D&C 67:____

248. "Let not your _____ turn _____ ; and when ye are worthy, in mine own
due time, ye shall see and know that which was conferred upon you by the
hands of my servant Joseph Smith, Jun. Amen." D&C 67:____

Section 68:

249. "And whatsoever they shall speak when moved upon by the Holy Ghost shall be
_____ , shall be the _____ of the Lord, shall be the _____ of
the Lord, shall be the _____ of the Lord, shall be the _____ of the Lord,
and the power of God unto salvation." D&C 68:___

250. Literal descendants of Aaron have a legal right to the bishopric, but there are
other conditions. "And a literal descendant of Aaron, also, must be
_____ by this Presidency, and found _____ , and
anointed, and ordained under the hands of this Presidency, otherwise they are
not legally authorized to officiate in their priesthood." D&C 68:___

251. If children are not taught to understand the doctrine of repentance, faith in
Christ, baptism, and the gift of the Holy Ghost when eight years old, the sin will
be upon the heads of the _____ . D&C 68:___

252. "Now, I, the Lord, am not well pleased with the inhabitants of Zion, for there are
_____ among them; and their children are also growing up in
wickedness; they also seek not _____ the riches of eternity."
D&C 68:___

Section 69:

253. John Whitmer was to travel with Oliver Cowdery to help protect the manuscript
and the monies he was carrying, but there was another reason. "Nevertheless,
let my servant John Whitmer travel many times from place to place, and from
church to church, that he may the more easily obtain _____ ."
D&C 69:___

Section 70:

254. "I, the Lord, have appointed them, and ordained them to be _____
over the revelations and commandments which I have given unto them, and
which I shall hereafter give unto them." D&C 70:___

Section 71:

255. "Wherefore, labor ye in my vineyard. Call upon the inhabitants of the earth, and bear record, and _____ the way for the _____ and _____ which are to come." D&C 71:____

Section 72:

256. "And verily in this thing ye have done wisely, for it is required of the Lord, at the hand of every steward, to render an account of his stewardship, both in _____ and in _____ ." D&C 72:____
257. "For he who is faithful and _____ in _____ is accounted worthy to inherit the mansions prepared for him of my Father." D&C 72:____
258. "The word of the Lord, in addition to the law which has been given, making known the duty of the _____ who has been ordained unto the church." D&C 72:____

Section 73:

259. "And then, behold, it shall be made known unto them, by the voice of the conference, their several _____ ." D&C 73:____

Section 74:

260. From the heading: Joseph "recommenced the translation of the Scriptures," and "... received the following, as an explanation of _____ ."
261. "But little children are _____ , being sanctified through the atonement of Jesus Christ; and this is what the scriptures mean." D&C 74:____

Section 75:

262. "And thus, if ye are faithful ye shall be laden with many _____ , and crowned with _____ , and glory, and immortality, and eternal life." D&C 75:____
263. "Calling on the name of the Lord for the Comforter, which shall teach them all things that are _____ for them." D&C 75:____

30

264. "And he who is faithful shall _____ all things, and shall be lifted up at the last day." D&C 75:____

Section 76:   Δ

265. From the heading: Joseph resumed the translation of the scriptures, and it was after he translated _____ that this vision was given.
266. "For by my _____ will I enlighten them, and by my _____ will I make known unto them the secrets of my will---yea, even those things which eye has not seen, nor ear heard, nor yet entered into the heart of man." D&C 76:____
267. Joseph and Sidney Rigdon received the vision together. They testified of the Son, "Of whom we bear record; and the record which we bear is the fulness of the gospel of Jesus Christ, who is the Son, whom we saw and with whom we _____ in the heavenly vision." D&C 76:____
268. "And now, after the many testimonies which have been given of him, this is the testimony, last of all, which we give of him: That ____ _____ !" D&C 76:____ ♣
269. Did God command them to write the vision while they were still under the influence of the Spirit? _____ D&C 76:____
270. They next received a vision of the sufferings of those with whom Lucifer made war and overcame.   The conclusion of this vision: "Wherefore, the end, the width, the height, the depth, and the misery thereof, they understand not, neither any man except those who are _____ unto this condemnation." D&C 76:____
271. The next vision was of those who would come forth in the resurrection of the just, who received the testimony of Jesus, were baptized, kept the commandments, and into whose hands the Father has given all things. "These are they whose bodies are _____ , whose glory is that of the sun, even the glory of God." D&C 76:____
272. They next saw the terrestrial world.   "These are they who are honorable men of the earth, who were _____ by the craftiness of men." D&C 76:____
273. "These are they who are not _____ in the testimony of Jesus; wherefore, they obtain not the crown over the kingdom of our God." D&C 76:____
274. They next saw the glory of the telestial. These are they who received not the gospel of Christ nor the testimony of Jesus. Do these also deny the Holy Spirit? _____ D&C 76:____

275. Do those in the telestial world differ one from another in glory, as one star differs from another star in glory? _____ D&C 76:____

276. "But great and marvelous are the works of the Lord, and the mysteries of his kingdom which he showed unto us, which surpass all understanding in _____ , and in _____ , and in _____ ." D&C 76:____

Section 77: ▲

277. From the heading: This revelation was given as an explanation of the _____ of St. John.

278. Is the sea of glass spoken of in Revelation 4:6 the earth? _____ D&C 77:____

279. "Their eyes are a representation of _____ and _____ , that is, they are full of knowledge; and their wings are a representation of _____ , to move, to act, etc." D&C 77:____

280. The book with seven seals concerns this earth during the seven thousand years of its continuance, or its _____ existence. D&C 77:____

281. The things in the 9th chapter of Revelation "are to be accomplished after the opening of the _____ seal, before the coming of Christ." D&C 77:____

Section 78:

282. "Who hath appointed Michael your prince, and established his feet, and set him upon high, and given unto him the keys of _____ under the counsel and direction of the Holy One." D&C 78:____

283. "And he that is a faithful and _____ steward shall inherit all things." D&C 78:____

Section 79:

284. "Wherefore, let your heart be _____ , my servant Jared Carter, and _____ not, saith your Lord, even Jesus Christ." D&C 79:____

Section 80:

285. "Therefore, declare the things which ye have heard, and verily _____ , and _____ to be true." D&C 80:____

Section 81:

286. "Wherefore, be faithful; stand in the office which I have appointed unto you; succor the weak, _____ _____ the hands which hang down, and _____ the feeble knees." D&C 81:____ ✦

Section 82:

287. "For of him unto whom much is _____ much is _____ ; and he who sins against the greater light shall receive the greater condemnation." D&C 82:____ ♣

288. "... unto that soul who sinneth shall the _____ sins return, saith the Lord your God." D&C 82:____

289. "I, the Lord, am _____ when ye do what I say; but when ye do not what I say, ye have no _____ ." D&C 82:____ ✦

290. "For Zion must increase in _____ , and in _____ ; her borders must be enlarged; her stakes must be strengthened; yea, verily I say unto you, Zion must _____ and put on her beautiful garments." D&C 82:___

Section 83:

291. "And the storehouse shall be kept by the consecrations of the church; and _____ and _____ shall be provided for, as also the poor." D&C 83:____

Section 84:   Δ

292. From the heading: The Prophet designates this revelation as a revelation on _____ .

293. "Which Abraham received the priesthood from _____ , who received it through the lineage of his fathers, even till Noah." D&C 84:___

294. "Which _____ continueth in the church of God in all generations, and is without beginning of days or end of years." D&C 84:___

295. "Therefore, in the _____ thereof, the power of godliness is manifest." D&C 84:___

296. "And the lesser priesthood continued, which priesthood holdeth the key of the _____ of angels and the _____ gospel."
D&C 84:___

297. How old was John (the Baptist) when he was ordained by the angel of God? _____ D&C 84:___

298. "For whoso is faithful unto the obtaining these two priesthoods of which I have spoken, and the magnifying their calling, are _____ by the Spirit unto the _____ of their bodies." D&C 84:___

299. "For he that receiveth my _____ receiveth me." D&C 84:___ ✦

300. "For the word of the Lord is _____ , and whatsoever is _____ is light, and whatsoever is light is Spirit, even the Spirit of Jesus Christ." D&C 84:___

301. "And your minds in times past have been darkened because of _____ , and because you have treated lightly the things you have received."
D&C 84:___ ♣

302. After giving the signs that shall follow them that believe, the Lord said, "But a commandment I give unto them, that they shall not _____ themselves of these things, neither speak them before the world." D&C 84:___

303. "And again I say unto you, my _____ , for from henceforth I shall call you _____ , it is expedient that I give unto you this commandment, that ye become even as my _____ in days when I was with them, traveling to preach the gospel in my power." D&C 84:___

304. "And any man that shall go and preach this gospel of the kingdom, and fail not to continue faithful in all things, shall not be _____ in mind, neither _____ , neither in body, limb, nor joint." D&C 84:___

305. "Neither take ye thought beforehand what ye shall say; but _____ up in your minds _____ the words of life, and it shall be given you in the very hour that portion that shall be meted unto every man." D&C 84:___ ♣

306. The concluding verse of the new song is, "Glory, and honor, and power, and might, Be ascribed to our God; for he is full of mercy, Justice, grace and truth, and _____ , Forever and ever, Amen." D&C 84:___

Section 85:

307. "And all those who are not found written in the book of _____ shall find none inheritance in that day." D&C 85:____

Section 86:

308. "Behold, verily I say unto you, the _____ are crying unto the Lord day and night, who are ready and waiting to be sent forth to reap down the fields." D&C 86:____

309. "Therefore, blessed are ye if ye continue in my goodness, a light unto the Gentiles, and through this priesthood, a _____ unto my people Israel." D&C 86:____

Section 87:   ▲

310. From the heading: This is a revelation and prophecy on _____ .

311. "Verily, thus saith the Lord concerning the wars that will shortly come to pass, beginning at the rebellion of _____ _____ ." D&C 87:____

312. "Wherefore, _____ ye in holy places, and be not _____ , until the day of the Lord come." D&C 87:____

Section 88:   Δ

313. From the heading: This revelation was designated by the Prophet as the "_____ _____ . . . plucked from the Tree of Paradise."

314. "And the light which shineth, which giveth you light, is through him who _____ your eyes, which is the same light that quickeneth your understandings." D&C 88:____

315. "And the _____ and the _____ are the soul of man." D&C 88:____ ✦

316. "For he who is not able to abide the _____ of a celestial kingdom cannot abide a celestial glory." D&C 88:____

317. Will the earth die and be quickened again? _____ D&C 88:____

318. "For what doth it profit a man if a gift is bestowed upon him, and he _____ not the gift? Behold, he rejoices not in that which is given unto him, neither rejoices in him who is the giver of the gift." D&C 88:____ ♣

319. "And again, verily I say unto you, that which is governed by _____ is also preserved by _____ and perfected and sanctified by the same." D&C 88:___ ✦

320. Speaking of the earth, sun, moon and stars, "Behold, all these are _____ , and any man who hath seen any or the least of these hath seen God moving in his majesty and power." D&C 88:___

321. "Draw _____ unto me and I will draw _____ unto you; seek me _____ and ye shall find me; ask, and ye shall receive; knock, and it shall be opened unto you." D&C 88:___ ✦

322. "Therefore, sanctify yourselves that your minds become single to God, and the days will come that you shall see him; for he will unveil his face unto you, and it shall be in his own _____ , and in his own _____ , and according to his own _____ ." D&C 88:___

323. "Teach ye diligently and my grace shall attend you, that you may be instructed more perfectly in _____ , in _____ , in _____ , in the _____ of the gospel, in all things that pertain unto the kingdom of God, that are expedient for you to understand." D&C 88:___ ♣

324. There are more things to be taught than in the previous verse. "Things both in _____ and in the _____ , and under the earth; things which have been, things which are, things which must shortly come to pass; things which are at home, things which are abroad." D&C 88:___

325. "He that seeketh me _____ shall find me, and shall not be forsaken." D&C 88:___ ✦

326. "Abide ye in the liberty wherewith ye are made free; _____ not yourselves in sin." D&C 88:___ ✦

327. The angels shall cry that the Bridegroom cometh ... "And immediately there shall appear a great _____ in heaven, and all people shall see it together." D&C 88:___

328. There shall be "_____ in heaven for the space of half an hour," then the curtain of heaven shall be unfolded, and the face of the Lord shall be unveiled. D&C 88:___

329. The saints who are alive shall be quickened and caught up to meet the Lord, there will be resurrections, seven angels, seven trumps, a final battle of Michael and his armies against the devil. Regarding what we should do now, "And as all have not faith, seek ye diligently and teach one another words of wisdom; yea, seek ye out of the best _____ words of wisdom; seek learning, even by _____ and also by _____ ." D&C 88:___ ♣

330. "_____ yourselves; prepare every needful thing; and establish a house, even a house of prayer, a house of fasting, a house of faith, a house of _____ , a house of glory, a house of _____ , a house of God." D&C 88:____ ♣

331. "Cease to be _____ ; cease to be _____ ; cease to find fault one with another; cease to _____ longer than is needful." D&C 88:____ ◆

332. "And above all things, clothe yourselves with the bond of _____ , as with a mantle, which is the bond of perfectness and peace." D&C 88:____

Section 89:   Δ

333. From the heading: This revelation is known as the _____ of _____ .

334. "Given for a principle with _____ , adapted to the capacity of the weak and the weakest of all saints, who are or can be called saints." D&C 89:____

335. "And, again, _____ _____ are not for the belly, but for the washing of your bodies." D&C 89:____

336. "And again, _____ is not for the body, neither for the belly, and is not good for man, but is an herb for bruises and all sick cattle, to be used with judgment and skill." D&C 89:____

337. Hot drinks are also not for the body or belly, but "... all wholesome _____ God hath ordained for the constitution, nature, and use of man." D&C 89:____

338. The flesh of beasts and the fowls of the air are "... ordained for the use of man with thanksgiving; nevertheless they are to be used _____ ." D&C 89:____

339. "All _____ is ordained for the use of man and of beasts, to be the staff of life." D&C 89:____

340. All saints who remember to keep and do these sayings, "... shall find wisdom and great _____ of knowledge, even hidden _____ ." D&C 89:____ ♣

341. "And shall run and not be _____ , and shall walk and not _____ ." D&C 89:____

Section 90:

342. "For it shall come to pass in that day, that every man shall hear the fulness of the gospel in his own _____ , and in his own _____ , through those who are ordained unto this power."   D&C 90:____

343. "And set in order the churches, and study and learn, and become acquainted with all good _____ , and with languages, tongues, and people."
     D&C 90:____

344. "Search _____ , pray _____ , and be _____ , and all things shall work together for your good, if ye walk uprightly and remember the covenant wherewith ye have covenanted one with another."   D&C 90:____   ♣

Section 91:

345. "Verily, thus saith the Lord unto you concerning the _____ ---There are many things contained therein that are true, and it is mostly translated correctly."   D&C 91:____

346. "There are many things contained therein that are not _____ , which are interpolations by the hands of men."   D&C 91:____

Section 92:

347. "And again, I say unto you my servant Frederick G. Williams, you shall be a _____ member in this order."   D&C 92:____

Section 93:   Δ

348. The record of John is quoted. He saw the glory of the Lord, that the worlds were made by him, that he was full of grace and truth. "And he received not of the fulness at first, but continued from _____ to _____ , until he received a fulness."   D&C 93:____

349. John saw the heavens opened and the Holy Ghost descend in the form of a dove upon the Son. "And he received all _____ , both in heaven and on earth, and the glory of the Father was with him."   D&C 93:____

350. After quoting from the record of John, the Lord said, "And it shall come to pass, that if you are faithful you shall receive the _____ of the record of John."   D&C 93:____

351. "And _____ is knowledge of things as they are, and as they were, and as they are to come."   D&C 93:____

352. "Man was also in the beginning with God. Intelligence, or the light of truth, was not _____ or made, neither indeed can be."   D&C 93:____

353. "All truth is _____ in that sphere in which God has placed it, to act for itself, as all intelligence also; otherwise there is no existence."   D&C 93:____ ♠

354. "For man is spirit. The elements are _____ , and spirit and element, inseparably connected, receive a fulness of joy."   D&C 93:____

355. "The glory of God is _____ , or, in other words, light and truth."   D&C 93:____ ✦

Section 94:

356. "And it shall be _____ unto the Lord from the foundation thereof, according to the order of the priesthood."   D&C 94:____

Section 95:

357. "They who are not chosen have sinned a very grievous sin, in that they are walking in _____ at noon-day."   D&C 95:____

358. "If you keep not my commandments, the _____ of the Father shall not continue with you, therefore you shall walk in darkness."   D&C 95:____

Section 96:

359. "For behold, verily I say unto you, this is the most expedient in me, that my word should go forth unto the children of men, for the purpose of _____ the hearts of the children of men for your good."   D&C 96:____

Section 97:

360. "For I, the Lord, will cause them to bring forth as a very fruitful _____ which is planted in a goodly land, by a pure stream, that yieldeth much precious fruit." D&C 97:____ 🌲

361. "And inasmuch as my people build a house unto me in the name of the Lord, and do not suffer any _____ thing to come into it, that it be not defiled, my glory shall rest upon it." D&C 97:____

362. "Therefore, verily, thus saith the Lord, let Zion rejoice, for this is Zion---THE _____ ____ _____ ; therefore, let Zion rejoice, while all the wicked shall mourn." D&C 97:____

Section 98:

363. "Therefore, he giveth this promise unto you, with an immutable covenant that they shall be fulfilled; and all things wherewith you have been _____ shall work together for your good, and to my name's glory, saith the Lord." D&C 98:____

364. "Therefore, renounce _____ and proclaim _____ , and seek diligently to turn the hearts of the children to their fathers, and the hearts of the fathers to the children." D&C 98:____

365. "And again, this is the law that I gave unto mine ancients, that they should not go out unto battle against any nation, kindred, tongue, or people, save I, the Lord, _____ them." D&C 98:____

Section 99:

366. "And who _____ you _____ me; and you shall have power to declare my word in the demonstration of my Holy Spirit." D&C 99:___

Section 100:

367. "Therefore, verily I say unto you, lift up your voices unto this people; speak the _____ that I shall put into your hearts, and you shall not be _____ before men." D&C 100:____

368. "But a commandment I give unto you, that ye shall declare whatsoever thing ye declare in my name, in _____ of heart, in the spirit of _____ , in all things."   D&C 100:____

369. "And I give unto you this _____ , that inasmuch as ye do this the Holy Ghost shall be shed forth in bearing record unto all things whatsoever ye shall say."   D&C 100:____

Section 101:

370. "They were _____ to hearken unto the voice of the Lord their God; therefore, the Lord their God is _____ to hearken unto their prayers, to answer them in the day of their trouble."   D&C 101:____

371. "They that remain, and are pure in heart, shall return, and come to their inheritances, they and their children, with songs of everlasting joy, to _____ _____ the waste places of Zion."   D&C 101:____

372. "And in that day the _____ of man, and the _____ of beasts, yea, the _____ of all flesh, shall cease from before my face."   D&C 101:____

373. "And in that day an infant shall not die until he is old; and his life shall be as the age of a _____ ."   D&C 101:____

374. When the Lord shall come he shall reveal all things. Will this include things of the past, such as the making of the earth (the things of the earth by which it was made)?   _____   D&C 101:____

375. "When men are called unto mine everlasting gospel, and covenant with an everlasting covenant, they are accounted as the _____ of the earth and the _____ of men."   D&C 101:____

376. "And for this purpose have I established the Constitution of this land, by the hands of _____ men whom I raised up unto this very purpose."   D&C 101:___

Section 102:

377. When a high council convenes to act upon a case, the accused has a right to one half of the council to prevent insult or injustice. "Those councilors who draw _____ numbers, that is, ____ , ____ , ____ , ____ , ____ , and ____ , are the individuals who are to stand up in behalf of the accused, and prevent insult and injustice."   D&C 102:____

41

Section 103:

378. "And by hearkening to observe all the words which I, the Lord their God, shall
     speak unto them, they shall never cease to _____ until the kingdoms
     of the world are subdued under my feet, and the earth is given unto the saints,
     to _____ it forever and ever." D&C 103:____
379. "All victory and glory is brought to pass unto you through your _____ ,
     faithfulness, and prayers of faith." D&C 103:____

Section 104:

380. "Verily I say unto you, my friends, I give unto you counsel, and a
     commandment, concerning all the properties which belong to the order which I
     commanded to be organized and established, to be a _____ order, and
     an everlasting order for the benefit of my church." D&C 104:____
381. "Therefore, inasmuch as some of my servants have not kept the commandment,
     but have broken the covenant through covetousness, and with _____
     words, I have cursed them with a very sore and grievous curse." D&C 104:____
382. "For the earth is full, and there is _____ and to spare; yea, I prepared all
     things, and have given unto the children of men to be _____ unto
     themselves." D&C 104:____
383. After appointing stewardships to several servants, the Lord says there will be
     two United Orders in two places. One shall be called the United Order of the
     Stake of Zion, the City of _____ [in Ohio]. The other shall be
     called the United Order of the City of _____ [in Missouri]. D&C 104:____
384. "And ye shall prepare for yourselves a place for a _____ , and
     consecrate it unto my name." D&C 104:____

Section 105:

385. "And Zion cannot be built up unless it is by the principles of the law of the
     _____ kingdom; otherwise I cannot receive her unto myself."
     D&C 105:____
386. The elders are told to wait for the redemption of Zion. "For behold, I do not
     require at their hands to fight the _____ of Zion; for, as I said in a
     former commandment, even so will I fulfil---I will fight your _____ ."
     D&C 105:____

387. The Lord cautions, "Talk not of judgments, neither _____ of faith nor of mighty works, but carefully gather together." D&C 105:___

388. The Lord's army is to first become very great, and sanctified, fair as the sun, clear as the moon, and her banners terrible unto all nations. [Therefore, by this light, not by force ...] "That the kingdoms of this world may be constrained to acknowledge that the kingdom of Zion is in very deed the kingdom of our God and his Christ; therefore, _____ ____ _____ _____ unto her laws." D&C 105:___

389. "And lift up an ensign of _____ , and make a proclamation of _____ unto the ends of the earth." D&C 105:___

Section 106:

390. "And again, verily I say unto you, there was joy in heaven when my servant Warren bowed to my scepter, and _____ himself from the crafts of men." D&C 106:___

Section 107:   ▲

391. Before the day of Melchizedek, the first Priesthood was called *the Holy Priesthood, after the* _____ *of the Son of God.* D&C 107:___

392. "The Melchizedek Priesthood holds the right of _____ , and has power and authority over all the offices in the church in all ages of the world, to administer in _____ things." D&C 107:___

393. The Priesthood of Aaron is called the lesser priesthood "... because it is an _____ to the greater, or the Melchizedek Priesthood, and has power in administering _____ ordinances." D&C 107:___

394. The Melchizedek Priesthood holds the keys of all the spiritual blessings of the Church. "To have the privilege of receiving the _____ of the kingdom of heaven, to have the heavens opened unto them." D&C 107:___

395. "The power and authority of the lesser, or Aaronic Priesthood, is to hold the keys of the _____ of angels, and to administer in outward ordinances, the _____ of the gospel, the baptism of repentance for the remission of sins." D&C 107:___

396. The presidency of the Church, the Twelve, the Seventy, and the high council quorums are explained. The lineage of the priesthood is given, as handed down by Adam from father to son. Three years previous to the death of Adam, he called his righteous posterity into the valley of _____ - _____ - _____ , and there bestowed upon them his last blessing. D&C 107:____

397. "And the Lord appeared unto them, and they rose up and blessed Adam, and called him _____ , the prince, the archangel." D&C 107:____

398. "These things were all written in the book of _____ , and are to be testified of in due time." D&C 107:____

399. The duties of the Twelve, of the elders, priests, teachers, deacons, bishops, councils, and presidents of quorums are given. In conclusion, "Wherefore, now let every man learn his _____ , and to act in the office in which he is appointed, in all diligence." D&C 107:____ ♣

400. "He that is _____ shall not be counted worthy to stand, and he that learns not his duty and shows himself not approved shall not be counted worthy to stand." D&C 107:____

Section 108:

401. "Therefore, strengthen your brethren in all your _____ , in all your prayers, in all your exhortations, and in all your doings." D&C 108:____ ♣

Section 109: ▲

402. From the heading: This revelation is the prayer offered at the dedication of the temple at _____ .

403. "For thou knowest that we have done this work through great tribulation; and out of our _____ we have given of our substance to build a house to thy name, that the Son of Man might have a place to _____ himself to his people." D&C 109:____

404. The Prophet pleads for deliverance from the yoke of lyings and slanderings against the people: "Break it off, O Lord; break it off from the necks of thy servants" (v. 33). To those in Missouri who have been driven from their lands, his heart goes out: "O Lord, how long wilt thou suffer this people to bear this affliction, and the cries of their _____ ones to ascend up in thine ears, and their blood come up in testimony before thee?" D&C 109:____

405. "Have mercy, O Lord, upon all the nations of the earth; have mercy upon the rulers of our land; may those principles, which were so honorably and nobly defended, namely, the _____ of our land, by our fathers, be established forever." D&C 109:____

406. He prays for kings, princes, the nobles, for all people, and the churches, all the poor, the needy, the afflicted, "That their hearts may be _____ when thy servants shall go out from thy house, O Jehovah, to bear testimony of thy name; that their _____ may give way before the truth." D&C 109:___

407. He asks for mercy on the children of Jacob, the children of Judah, the scattered remnants of Israel, himself, his family, their connections, the presidents of the Church and their families. "Remember all thy church, O Lord, with all their families, and all their immediate connections, with all their _____ and _____ ones, with all the poor and meek of the earth." D&C 109:___

408. "O hear, O hear, O hear us, O Lord! And answer these petitions, and accept the dedication of this house unto thee, the _____ of our hands, which we have _____ unto thy name." D&C 109:____

Section 110:   ▲

409. From the heading: These visions were manifested to Joseph Smith and Oliver Cowdery in the _____ at Kirtland, Ohio, April 3, 1836.

410. The veil was taken from their minds, and they saw the Lord standing upon the breastwork of the _____ . D&C 110:____

411. "His _____ were as a flame of fire; the hair of his head was white like the pure snow; his _____ shone above the brightness of the sun; and his _____ was as the sound of the rushing of great waters."
D&C 110:____

412. "After this vision closed, the heavens were again opened unto us; and _____ appeared before us, and committed unto us the keys of the gathering of Israel from the four parts of the earth." D&C 110:____

413. "After this, _____ appeared, and committed the dispensation of the gospel of Abraham." D&C 110:____

414. "After this vision had closed, another great and glorious vision burst upon us; for _____ the prophet, who was taken to heaven without tasting death, stood before us." D&C 110:____

Section 111:

415. "Therefore, be ye as wise as serpents and yet without sin; and I will order all things for your good, as fast as ye are able to _____ them."
D&C 111:____

Section 112:

416. "Contend thou, therefore, morning by morning; and day after day let thy warning voice go forth; and when the night cometh let not the inhabitants of the earth _____ , because of thy speech." D&C 112:____
417. "Be thou _____ ; and the Lord thy God shall lead thee by the hand, and give thee answer to thy prayers." D&C 112:____ ✦

Section 113:

418. From the heading: This section contains answers to certain questions on the writings of _____ .
419. Who is the stem of Jesse? _____ . D&C 113:____
420. To put on her strength is to put on the _____ of the priesthood.
D&C 113:____
421. If the scattered remnants return to the Lord from whence they have fallen, "... the promise of the Lord is that he will speak to them, or give them _____ ." D&C 113:____

Section 114:

422. "For verily thus saith the Lord, that inasmuch as there are those among you who deny my name, others shall be _____ in their stead and receive their bishopric." D&C 114:____

Section 115:

423. "For thus shall my church be called in the last days, even _____ _____ ____ _____ _____ ___ _____ - _____ _____ ."
D&C 115:____

46

Section 116:

424. "Spring Hill is named by the Lord Adam-ondi-Ahman, because, said he, it is the place where _____ shall come to visit his people, or the _____ of Days shall sit, as spoken of by Daniel the Prophet." D&C 116:____

Section 117:

425. "Is there not room enough on the mountains of Adam-ondi-Ahman, and on the plains of Olaha Shinehah, or the land where Adam dwelt, that you should covet that which is but the _____ , and neglect the more _____ matters?" D&C 117:____

Section 118:

426. "Let my servant John _____ , and also my servant John E. _____ , and also my servant Wilford _____ , and also my servant Willard _____ , be appointed to fill the places of those who have fallen." D&C 118:____

Section 119:

427. From the heading: "The law of _____ , as understood today, had not been given to the Church previous to this revelation."
428. "And I say unto you, if my people observe not this law, to keep it holy, and by this law _____ the land of Zion unto me, that my statutes and my judgments may be kept thereon, that it may be most holy, behold, verily I say unto you, it shall not be a land of Zion unto you." D&C 119:____

Section 120:

429. The properties tithed "shall be disposed of by a council, composed of the _____ Presidency of my Church, and of the _____ and his council, and by my high council; and by mine own voice unto them, saith the Lord." D&C 120:____

430. From the heading: This section is the prayer and prophecies written by Joseph Smith the Prophet, while he was a prisoner in the jail at _____ , Missouri.

431. "Yea, O Lord, how long shall they suffer these wrong and unlawful oppressions, before thine heart shall be _____ toward them, and thy bowels be moved with compassion toward them?" D&C 121:____

432. "My son, peace be unto thy soul; thine adversity and thine afflictions shall be but a _____ moment." D&C 121:____

433. "Thou are not yet as _____ ; thy friends do not contend against thee, neither charge thee with transgression, as they did _____ ." D&C 121:____

434. "But those who cry _____ do it because they are the servants of sin, and are the children of disobedience themselves." D&C 121:____

435. "God shall give unto you _____ by his Holy Spirit, yea, by the unspeakable gift of the Holy Ghost, that has not been _____ since the world was until now." D&C 121:____

436. "How long can rolling waters remain impure? What power shall stay the heavens? As well might man stretch forth his puny arm to stop the _____ river in its decreed course, or to turn it up stream, as to hinder the Almighty from pouring down _____ from heaven upon the heads of the Latter-day Saints." D&C 121:____

437. Those who are not chosen do not learn this one lesson--- "That the rights of the priesthood are inseparably connected with the powers of heaven, and that the powers of heaven cannot be controlled nor handled only upon the principles of _____ ." D&C 121:____

438. When we undertake to cover our sins, to gratify our pride, or to exercise control or dominion or compulsion, in any degree of unrighteousness, "behold, the heavens withdraw themselves; the Spirit of the Lord is grieved; and when it is withdrawn, Amen to the _____ or the _____ of that man." D&C 121:____

439. "We have learned by sad experience that it is the nature and disposition of almost all men, as soon as they get a little authority, as they suppose, they will immediately begin to exercise unrighteous _____ ." D&C 121:____

440. "No power or influence can or ought to be maintained by virtue of the priest- hood, only by _____ , by long-suffering, by _____ and meekness, and by _____ unfeigned." D&C 121:____ ♣

441. "Reproving betimes with sharpness, when moved upon by the Holy Ghost; and then showing forth afterwards an increase of _____ ." D&C 121:___

442. "Let thy bowels also be full of charity towards all men, and to the household of faith, and let _____ garnish thy thoughts unceasingly; then shall thy _____ wax strong in the presence of God; and the doctrine of the priesthood shall distil upon thy soul as the dews from heaven." D&C 121:___ ♣

443. "The Holy Ghost shall be thy constant companion, and thy scepter an unchanging scepter of righteousness and truth; and thy dominion shall be an everlasting dominion, and without _____ means it shall _____ unto thee forever and ever." D&C 121:___

Section 122:   ▲

444. From the heading: Where was Joseph when he received this revelation?

_____

445. "The ends of the earth shall inquire after thy name, and _____ shall have thee in derision, and hell shall rage against thee." D&C 122:___

446. "... if the very jaws of hell shall gape open the mouth wide after thee, know thou, my son, that all these things shall give thee _____ , and shall be for thy good." D&C 122:___

447. "The Son of Man hath _____ below them all. Art thou greater than he?" D&C 122:___

Section 123:   ▲

448. From the heading: Where was Joseph when he received this revelation?

_____

449. "For there are many yet on the earth among all sects, parties, and denominations, who are blinded by the _____ craftiness of men, whereby they lie in wait to deceive, and who are only kept from the _____ because they know not where to find it." D&C 123:___

450. "Therefore, dearly beloved brethren, let us _____ do all things that lie in our power; and then may we stand still, with the utmost assurance, to see the salvation of God." D&C 123:___

Section 124:

451. From the heading: This revelation was given at _____ , Illinois.

452. The Lord tells Joseph, "... for unto this end have I raised you up, that I might show forth my wisdom through the _____ things of the earth." D&C 124:___

453. The Lord says that a proclamation is to be made to all the kings of the world, to the president-elect, the governors and all the nations of the earth. "Call ye, therefore, upon them with loud proclamation, and with your testimony, fearing them not, for they are as _____ , and all their glory as the flower thereof which soon falleth." D&C 124:____

454. "And again, verily I say unto you, blessed is my servant Hyrum Smith; for I, the Lord, love him because of the _____ of his heart, and because he _____ that which is right before me, saith the Lord." D&C 124:___

455. A house is to be built [later called the Nauvoo House], "And it shall be for a house for boarding, a house that strangers may come from afar to lodge therein; therefore let it be a _____ house, worthy of all acceptation, that the weary traveler may find health and safety while he shall _____ the word of the Lord." D&C 124:____

456. A house [the Nauvoo Temple] is to be built from the precious things of the earth, where the Lord may come and restore that which was lost. And, "For a baptismal font there is not upon the earth, that they, my saints, may be baptized for those who are _____ ." D&C 124:___

457. In this house, the Lord will reveal his ordinances. And, "For I deign to reveal unto my church things which have been kept hid from before the foundation of the world, things that pertain to the _____ of the fulness of times." D&C 124:____

458. From the temple, the Lord turns again to the boarding house, giving the name as the Nauvoo House. The manner of selling stock in the house, and who should put stock into it, are given, with mention of many servants. Hyrum may take the office of Priesthood and Patriarch, which was appointed unto him by his father, to hold the keys of the patriarchal blessings upon the heads of all the people. "And from this time forth I appoint unto him that he may be a _____ , and a _____ , and a _____ unto my church, as well as my servant Joseph." D&C 124:___

459. William Law shall heal the sick and cast out devils, "And he shall be led in paths where the poisonous serpent cannot lay hold upon his heel, and he shall mount up in the _____ of his thoughts as upon eagles' wings." D&C 124:___

460. William, Sidney, and others are counseled in their labors. The Lord turns again to Hyrum's calling as a patriarch, to hold the sealing blessing; then, "I give unto you my servant Joseph to be a _____ elder over all my church, to be a _____ , a revelator, a seer, and prophet." D&C 124:____

461. "I give unto you my servant _____ _____ to be a president over the Twelve traveling council." D&C 124:____

Section 125:

462. Concerning the Saints in the Territory of Iowa, "Let them build up a city unto my name upon the land opposite the city of Nauvoo, and let the name of _____ be named upon it." D&C 125:____

Section 126:

463. "Dear and _____ - _____ brother, Brigham Young, verily thus saith the Lord unto you: My servant Brigham, it is no more required at your hand to leave your family as in times past." D&C 126:____

Section 127:

464. From the heading: This section is an epistle from Joseph Smith, containing directions on _____ for the _____ .

465. "And as for the perils which I am called to pass through, they seem but a _____ thing to me, as the envy and wrath of man have been my common lot all the days of my life." D&C 127:____

466. "Verily, thus saith the Lord unto you concerning your dead: When any of you are baptized for your dead, let there be a _____ , and let him be eye-witness of your baptisms." D&C 127:____

467. "I will say to all the _____ , that I desired, with exceedingly great desire, to have addressed them from the stand on the subject of baptism for the dead, on the following Sabbath." D&C 127:____

Section 128: ▲

468. "As I stated to you in my letter before I left my place, that I would write to you from time to time and give you information in relation to many subjects, I now resume the subject of the _____ for the _____ ." D&C 128:____

469. Joseph writes more about the recorders; then, to remember that John the Revelator was contemplating this very subject in relation to the dead, as recorded in Revelation ____ : ____ .

470. The book of _____ is the record which is kept in heaven. D&C 128:____

471. "It may seem to some to be a very bold doctrine that we talk of---a power which records or _____ on earth and _____ in heaven. Nevertheless, in all ages of the world, whenever the Lord has given a dispensation of the priest-hood to any man by actual revelation, or any set of men, this _____ has always been given." D&C 128:____

472. For the precedent, Matthew ____ : ____ , ____ is quoted. D&C 128:____

473. "Consequently, the baptismal font was instituted as a similitude of the _____ ." D&C 128:____

474. After scriptures from 1 Corinthians 15, Joseph quotes Malachi, last chapter, verses ____ and ____ .

475. "Now, what do we hear in the gospel which we have received? A voice of _____ ! A voice of _____ from heaven; and a voice of truth out of the earth." D&C 128:____

476. Who detected the devil when he appeared as an angel of light, on the banks of the Susquehanna? _____ D&C 128:____

477. "And the voice of Michael, the archangel; the voice of Gabriel, and of _____ , and of divers angels, from Michael or Adam down to the pre-sent time, all declaring their dispensation, their rights, their keys, their honors, their majesty and glory, and the power of their priesthood." D&C 128:____

478. "Brethren, shall we not go on in so great a cause? Go _____ and not _____ . Courage, brethren; and on, on to the victory!" D&C 128:____ ♣

Section 129: ▲

479. When you shake hands with an angel who is a messenger from God, will you be able to feel his hand? _____ D&C 129:____

Section 130: ▲

480. "And that same _____ which exists among us here will exist among us there, only it will be coupled with eternal glory." D&C 130:____

481. "Whatever principle of _____ we attain unto in this life, it will rise with us in the resurrection." D&C 130:____ ✦

482. "And if a person gains more knowledge and intelligence in this life through his _____ and _____ than another, he will have so much the advantage in the world to come." D&C 130:____

483. "And when we obtain any _____ from God, it is by obedience to that law upon which it is predicated." D&C 130:____ ✦

484. "The Father has a body of flesh and bones as _____ as man's; the Son also; but the Holy Ghost has not a body of flesh and bones." D&C 130:___

Section 131: ▲

485. "In the celestial glory there are _____ heavens or degrees." D&C 131:____

486. "It is impossible for a man to be saved in _____ ." D&C 131:____ ✦

487. "There is no such thing as immaterial matter. All spirit is _____ , but it is more fine or pure, and can only be discerned by purer eyes." D&C 131:____

Section 132: Δ

488. "For behold, I reveal unto you a new and an everlasting _____ ." D&C 132:____

489. "For all who will have a _____ at my hands shall abide the law which was appointed for that _____ , and the conditions thereof, as were instituted from before the foundation of the world." D&C 132:____

490. Must a covenant of marriage be sealed by the Holy Spirit of promise, through him anointed and appointed unto this power, for it to be valid and in force when out of the world? _____ D&C 132:____

491. "Then shall they be _____ , because they have no end; therefore shall they be from everlasting to everlasting, because they continue." D&C 132:____

492. Will blasphemy against the Holy Ghost ever be forgiven? _____ D&C 132:___

493. "God commanded Abraham, and _____ gave Hagar to Abraham to wife. And why did she do it? Because this was the _____ ." D&C 132:____

494. Did David fall from his exaltation? _____ D&C 132:____

495. Concerning Emma Smith, "And again, verily I say, let mine handmaid forgive my servant Joseph his trespasses; and then shall she be forgiven her trespasses, wherein she has trespassed against me; and I, the Lord thy God, will bless her, and multiply her, and make her heart to _____ ." D&C 132:____

Section 133:   Δ

496. From the heading: Note the date. This section is out of chronological order. It was first added to the book of Doctrine and Covenants as an _____ , and was subsequently assigned a section number.
497. "Wherefore, _____ ye, _____ ye, O my people; sanctify yourselves; gather ye together, O ye people of my church." D&C 133:____
498. "Go ye out from _____ . Be ye clean that bear the vessels of the Lord." D&C 133:____ ✦
499. "Send forth the elders of my church unto the _____ which are afar off; unto the islands of the sea; send forth unto foreign lands; call upon all nations." D&C 133:____
500. "But verily, thus saith the Lord, let not your flight be in _____ , but let all things be prepared before you; and he that goeth, let him not look _____ lest sudden destruction shall come upon him." D&C 133:____
501. Will the earth be like as it was in the days before it was divided? _____ D&C 133:____
502. "And the Lord, even the Savior, shall stand in the midst of his people, and shall _____ over all flesh." D&C 133:____
503. Will pools of living water come forth from the barren deserts? _____ D&C 133:____
504. "And the Lord shall be _____ in his apparel, and his garments like him that treadeth in the wine-vat." D&C 133:____
505. "And for this cause, that men might be made partakers of the glories which were to be revealed, the Lord sent forth the fulness of his gospel, his everlasting covenant, reasoning in _____ and _____ ." D&C 133:____

Section 134:   Δ

506. From the heading: This section is a declaration of belief regarding _____ and _____ in general.

507. "We believe that _____ were instituted of God for the benefit of man; and that he holds men accountable for their acts in relation to them, both in _____ laws and administering them." D&C 134:____ 🌲

508. "We believe that all men are bound to _____ and _____ the respective governments in which they reside." D&C 134:____

509. Do we believe in the free exercise of religious belief? _____ D&C 134:____

510. Do we believe it just to mingle religious influence with civil government? _____ D&C 134:____

511. Do we believe that the most a religious society has a right to do, in dealing with members for disorderly conduct, is to excommunicate them and withdraw from them their fellowship? _____ D&C 134:____

Section 135:   ▲

512. From the heading: "This document was written by Elder _____ _____ of the Council of the Twelve, who was a witness to the events."

513. On what date were Joseph and Hyrum shot? _____ D&C 135:____

514. "Joseph Smith, the Prophet and Seer of the Lord, has done more, save _____ only, for the salvation of men in this world, than any other man that ever lived in it." D&C 135:____

515. "Hyrum Smith was _____ - _____ years old in February, 1844, and Joseph Smith was _____ - _____ in December, 1843." D&C 135:____

Section 136:   ▲

516. From the heading: This revelation is the word and will of the Lord, given through President _____ _____ .

517. "The Word and Will of the Lord concerning the Camp of Israel in their journeyings to the _____ ." D&C 136:____

518. "Let the companies be organized with captains of _____ , captains of _____ , and captains of _____ ." D&C 136:____

519. "Let each company bear an equal proportion, according to the dividend of their property, in taking the _____ , the _____ , the _____ , and the families of those who have gone into the army." D&C 136:____

520. "I am he who led the children of Israel out of the land of Egypt; and my arm is stretched out in the last days, to save my people _____ ." D&C 136:____

521. "Thou shalt be diligent in _____ what thou hast, that thou mayest be a wise steward; for it is the free gift of the Lord thy God." D&C 136:____

522. "If thou art merry, praise the Lord with _____ , with _____ , with _____ , and with a prayer of praise and thanksgiving." D&C 136:____

Section 137: ▲

523. From the heading: Note the date. This revelation is out of chronological order. It is a vision given to Joseph Smith in the temple at _____ , _____ .

524. He saw the celestial kingdom and the glory thereof, the beauty of the gate, the blazing throne of God, and the beautiful streets. He saw Father Adam, Abraham, his father and mother, and his brother _____ . D&C 137:____

525. "Thus came the voice of the Lord unto me, saying: All who have died without a knowledge of this gospel, who would have received it if they had been permitted to tarry, shall be heirs of the _____ kingdom of God." D&C 137:____

526. "For I, the Lord, will judge all men according to their works, according to the _____ of their _____ ." D&C 137:____ ✦

527. "And I also beheld that all children who die before they arrive at the years of accountability are saved in the _____ kingdom of heaven." D&C 138:____

Section 138: Δ

528. From the heading: This vision was given to President _____ in Salt Lake City, Utah, on October 3, 1918.

529. "I opened the Bible and read the _____ and _____ chapters of the first epistle of Peter, and as I read I was greatly _____ ." D&C 138:___

530. "As I pondered over these things which are written, the eyes of my understanding were opened, and the Spirit of the Lord rested upon me, and I saw the hosts of the _____ , both small and great." D&C 138:____

531. The Son of God appeared to the vast multitude, and preached to them the everlasting gospel. Did he go to the wicked and ungodly and unrepentant? _____ D&C 138:___

532. "But behold, from among the righteous, he _____ his forces and appointed messengers, clothed with power and authority, and commissioned them to go forth and carry the light of the gospel to them that were in darkness, even to all the spirits of men; and thus was the gospel preached to the _____ ." D&C 138:____

533. In this vast congregation he saw Father Adam and Mother Eve, with many of her faithful daughters who had lived throughout the ages. Abel, Seth, Noah, and many others are mentioned down to the present time, who were among the noble and great ones chosen in the beginning. "Even before they were born, they, with many others, received their first _____ in the world of spirits and were _____ to come forth in the due time of the Lord." D&C 138:____

534. "I beheld that the faithful elders of this dispensation, when they depart from mortal life, continue their labors in the _____ of the gospel of repentance and redemption." D&C 138:____

535. "The dead who _____ will be redeemed, through obedience to the ordinances of the house of God." D&C 138:____

Official Declarations:

536. Official Declaration---1 was given by _____ _____ , President of the Church of Jesus Christ of Latter-day Saints.

537. Official Declaration---1 was sustained by the Church in General Conference in Salt Lake City, Utah, October 6, _____ .

538. Official Declaration---2 was presented on September 30, _____ , at the 148th Semiannual General Conference of The Church of Jesus Christ of Latter-day Saints.

539. "In early June of this year, the First Presidency announced that a revelation had been received by President _____ extending priesthood and temple blessings to all worthy male members of the Church."

Color-in graphic for expedition progress

The color-in graphic **DOCTRINE AND COVENANTS** on the following page is to mark your progress and serve as a symbol as you move through the Captain's Log. Color the appropriate part of each letter for each section completed. Use an orange or gold-colored pencil, symbolic of light and truth. Through the light and truth of modern revelation in the Doctrine and Covenants, the restored gospel of Jesus Christ is manifest. All of the sections combine into words of life, and will glow more brightly in your life, step by step, little by little, as you advance through your study and reach your milestones.

This graphic also signifies that those who travel the path to Christ must know the gospel (the doctrine) and then enter into promises (covenants) to live according to the will of the Lord. For example, the first covenant is established by the ordinance of baptism. To those who enter into and honor these covenants the Lord in turn promises blessings or treasures. These covenants between God and his children must be performed by authorized representatives of the Lord. The symbol is that we come unto Christ (on the left) through the doctrines and covenants of the gospel and the help of God's servants (on the right, represented by Joseph Smith).

You may photocopy this graphic to preserve the original, then keep it in a handy place to highlight your progress.

Milestones and rewards

Three milestones are defined on page 61, which divide The Doctrine and Covenants into three parts as you work your way through the Captain's Log. Like the milestone markers on a mountain road, they define progress and a chance for celebration---a place to stop and refresh yourself. Decide upon a reward for each milestone, and write it in the space provided at the right.

Suggestions for rewards are on page 62. You can define whatever rewards you want. For children, the rewards should be discussed and agreed upon with parents. If you are doing this study on your own, you may reward yourself, but in general these are between people as a demonstration of encouragement and support.

The more lasting rewards, of course, are the knowledge and testimony to be received as gifts from the Lord. However, there is no harm in using additional rewards to mark progress. In this small way we can learn to impart one to another (D&C 88:124), to lift each other (D&C 81:5), and to form a bond of charity (D&C 124:125).

Milestone record

The milestone record on page 63 is your official documentation of progress. Enter the dates of completion of each section. Completion is defined as both reading a section and answering the questions in the Captain's Log. The sections are divided into three groups here to correspond with your milestones and rewards. You may photocopy this page for easier access.

Milestones

Rewards

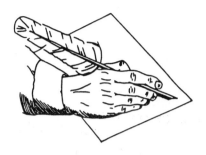

(Record a reward for each milestone. See page 62 for suggestions.)

Milestone 1: Sections 1 - 40   Reward:

Milestone 2: Sections 41 - 89   Reward:

Milestone 3: Sections 90 - 138   Reward:

Reward suggestions for each milestone

> *But, behold, I say unto you, that you must __study__ it out in your mind; then you must ask me if it be right, and if it is right I will cause that your bosom shall burn within you; therefore, you shall feel that it is right.*
> *. . . therefore, you cannot __write__ that which is sacred save it be given you from me.*   *(D&C 9:8-9)*

Milestone 1: Sections 1 through 40

Reward: study materials

- marking pencils, pens, notebooks
- briefcase or carrying bag
- a good book
- a new desk or chair
- scripture software for computers

> *All __wholesome__ herbs God hath ordained for the constitution, nature, and use of man---*
> *All grain is good for the __food__ of man; as also the fruit of the vine; that which yieldeth fruit, whether in the ground or above the ground---*
> *(D&C 89:10,16)*

Milestone 2: Sections 41 through 89

Reward: wholesome food

- eat out at a restaurant
- specially prepared meal
- case of favorite (wholesome) cereals
- case of favorite fruit or fruit juice

> *Let each company provide themselves with all the teams, wagons, __provisions__, clothing, and other necessaries for the journey, that they can.*   *(D&C 136:5)*

Milestone 3: Sections 90 through 138

Reward: provisions for the "journey" ahead

- missionary provisions: appropriate deposit into a missionary savings account, scriptures, clothing
- college provisions: appropriate deposit into a college savings account
- other provisions: clothing, musical supplies, fund for temple trip, a college course

Milestone Record -- enter dates of completion

First Milestone	Second Milestone	Third Milestone
1 _____	41 _____	90 _____
2 _____	42 _____	91 _____
3 _____	43 _____	92 _____
4 _____	44 _____	93 _____
5 _____	45 _____	94 _____
6 _____	46 _____	95 _____
7 _____	47 _____	96 _____
8 _____	48 _____	97 _____
9 _____	49 _____	98 _____
10 _____	50 _____	99 _____
11 _____	51 _____	100 _____
12 _____	52 _____	101 _____
13 _____	53 _____	102 _____
14 _____	54 _____	103 _____
15 _____	55 _____	104 _____
16 _____	56 _____	105 _____
17 _____	57 _____	106 _____
18 _____	58 _____	107 _____
19 _____	59 _____	108 _____
20 _____	60 _____	109 _____
21 _____	61 _____	110 _____
22 _____	62 _____	111 _____
23 _____	63 _____	112 _____
24 _____	64 _____	113 _____
25 _____	65 _____	114 _____
26 _____	66 _____	115 _____
27 _____	67 _____	116 _____
28 _____	68 _____	117 _____
29 _____	69 _____	118 _____
30 _____	70 _____	119 _____
31 _____	71 _____	120 _____
32 _____	72 _____	121 _____
33 _____	73 _____	122 _____
34 _____	74 _____	123 _____
35 _____	75 _____	124 _____
36 _____	76 _____	125 _____
37 _____	77 _____	126 _____
38 _____	78 _____	127 _____
39 _____	79 _____	128 _____
40 _____	80 _____	129 _____
	81 _____	130 _____
	82 _____	131 _____
	83 _____	132 _____
	84 _____	133 _____
	85 _____	134 _____
	86 _____	135 _____
	87 _____	136 _____
	88 _____	137 _____
	89 _____	138 _____

Collecting diamonds

Diamonds are the hardest naturally-occurring substance known to man. The word comes from the Greek *adamas*, meaning "the invincible," and refers to the diamond's hard, brilliant lustre. In the symbolism of gemstones, the diamond represents steadfast love and is the birthstone for April. A properly cut diamond will reflect a greater amount of light to the eye of the observer than will a gem of lesser refractive power, and will thus appear more brilliant. The high rate of dispersion gives diamonds their "fire," which is caused by the separation of white light into the colors of the spectrum as it passes through the stone.

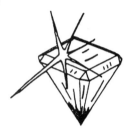

So too are the *diamonds* you will collect from the scriptures. Scriptures are invincible; they represent the steadfast love of the Lord, and they shine with brilliant fire as light passes through them into your soul. You will be the diamond cutter who deftly produces the flat faces, so that the light is broken into its colors. These are the inspired interpretations that you cut from the scriptures when you mark, memorize, and ponder them. These facets, in combination with the brilliant lustre of the crystal, will cause your *diamonds* to sparkle and glitter.

In addition, scripture *diamonds* are like the pure crystal of the Urim and Thummim, through which the Lord's servants receive revelation. See *Where is the Urim and Thummim today?* on page 96.

You will be marking *diamond* scriptures with a red symbol (see below). Why red? Actually, some diamonds really are red (although rare). In nature, most gem diamonds are transparent and nearly colorless. But a "fancy" diamond has a distinct body color; red, blue, and green are rarest, and orange, violet, yellow, and yellowish green more common. Red is chosen from among these colors because red is brilliant, alive, and the color of love. (And, of course, red marking pencils are easily available!) An actual red diamond gem is mostly transparent, but with a high refractive power that separates white light into a pale but brilliant red as it passes through the stone, giving the diamond lustre and fire. Your red *diamond* scriptures will likewise refract heavenly light into iridescent beauty, and touch your heart with an ember of light.

How to collect diamond scriptures:

There are 32 *diamond* scriptures you may collect in this expedition. These are identified in four places: the *diamond* symbol (◆) in the Captain's Log (pp. 5-57), the boxed *diamond* scriptures (pp. 66-69), the *diamond* table (p. 71), and the color-in graphics (pp. 73-74).

You "collect" a *diamond* scripture by memorizing it, then marking it in your scriptures. You have memorized a scripture when you can recite it to someone, including the reference. Why the reference? A true explorer knows where his treasures were discovered. Can you imagine someone showing you a great discovery and not knowing where it came from? Knowing its origin is half its value.

To assist in memorizing, you may photocopy the boxed scriptures on pages 66-69, then cut out or paste to cards. Use these for review, for recital at family home evenings, etc. Also see *Why memorize?* on page 94.

To mark a *diamond* scripture:

1. Enter a red diamond (◇) in the margin next to the scripture, or if you prefer two arrows back to back (<>), with a red colored pencil, to signify the diamond.

2. Highlight the scripture with a colored pencil, such as by underscoring or shading. This marking need not be in red, since the diamond symbol in the margin is in red. Because a *diamond* may not include every word in a scripture, highlight only the words of the *diamond*; that is, the words you will memorize. Refer to pages 66-69 to see the suggested words for each *diamond*.

3. Enter the scripture information in the *diamond* table (p. 71) that you will insert into your scriptures. The scripture reference and key words for 32 *diamonds* are already entered in the table. All you have to do at this point is enter the date for the given scripture to indicate you have memorized and marked it. You may enter the association portion of the table later. See page 70. This table is important because you can always refer to it to find your *diamonds*, and it will help in reviewing your memorizations.

After memorizing and marking a *diamond* scripture, go to the color-in graphics on pages 73-74. Color (in red) the appropriate letter that matches the given scripture, to signify that you have collected this treasure and put it into your pouch, that you have preserved it for the journey home from this expedition.

How are diamond scriptures different from tree scriptures (p. 75)?

Compared to *tree* scriptures, *diamonds* are shorter verses. That's all. You may want to collect these first. They are small and beautiful. They are easy to pick up and put in your pouch.

✦ *Diamond* scriptures:

For I the Lord cannot look upon sin with the least degree of allowance.

D&C 1:31 ✦

Did I not speak peace to your mind concerning the matter? What greater witness can you have than from God?

D&C 6:23 ✦

For God doth not walk in crooked paths, neither doth he turn to the right hand nor to the left.

D&C 3:2 ✦

Look unto me in every thought; doubt not, fear not.

D&C 6:36 ✦

For, behold, you should not have feared man more than God.

D&C 3:7 ✦

Do not run faster or labor more than you have strength and means provided.

D&C 10:4 ✦

Trifle not with sacred things.

D&C 6:12 ✦

Remember the worth of souls is great in the sight of God.

D&C 18:10 ✦

And gave unto him commandments which inspired him.

D&C 20:7 ✦

And that ye may not be deceived seek ye earnestly the best gifts, always remembering for what they are given.

D&C 46:8 ✦

For my soul delighteth in the song of the heart; yea, the song of the righteous is a prayer unto me.

D&C 25:12 ✦

And that which doth not edify is not of God, and is darkness.

D&C 50:23 ✦

But if ye are prepared ye shall not fear.

D&C 38:30 ✦

For after much tribulation come the blessings.

D&C 58:4 ✦

And the Spirit shall be given unto you by the prayer of faith; and if ye receive not the Spirit ye shall not teach.

D&C 42:14 ✦

Behold, he who has repented of his sins, the same is forgiven, and I, the Lord, remember them no more.

D&C 58:42 ✦

Succor the weak, lift up the hands which hang down, and strengthen the feeble knees.

D&C 81:5 ◆

That which is governed by law is also preserved by law and perfected and sactified by the same.

D&C 88:34 ◆

I, the Lord, am bound when ye do what I say; but when ye do not what I say, ye have no promise.

D&C 82:10 ◆

Draw near unto me and I will draw near unto you; seek me diligently and ye shall find me.

D&C 88:63 ◆

For he that receiveth my servants receiveth me.

D&C 84:36 ◆

He that seeketh me early shall find me, and shall not be forsaken.

D&C 88:83 ◆

And the spirit and the body are the soul of man.

D&C 88:15 ◆

Abide ye in the liberty wherewith ye are made free; entangle not yourselves in sin.

D&C 88:86 ◆

Cease to be idle; cease to be unclean; cease to find fault one with another; cease to sleep longer than is needful.

D&C 88:124 ✦

And when we obtain any blessing from God, it is by obedience to that law upon which it is predicated.

D&C 130:21 ✦

The glory of God is intelligence, or, in other words, light and truth.

D&C 93:36 ✦

It is impossible for a man to be saved in ignorance.

D&C 131:6 ✦

Be thou humble; and the Lord thy God shall lead thee by the hand, and give thee answer to thy prayers.

D&C 112:10 ✦

Go ye out from Babylon. Be ye clean that bear the vessels of the Lord.

D&C 133:5 ✦

Whatever principle of intelligence we attain unto in this life, it will rise with us in the resurrection.

D&C 130:18 ✦

For I, the Lord, will judge all men according to their works, according to the desire of their hearts.

D&C 137:9 ✦

The diamond table:

You may photocopy page 71, and from this cut out the table. Fold at the middle, then insert the table inside the front or back cover of your scriptures. If you have a larger or smaller edition of scriptures, fit to size by using the "enlarge" or "reduce" option of the copier when making the photocopy.

This table is the "pouch" into which you put your *diamonds* so you don't lose them. You can always come here when you want to bring out a *diamond* and enjoy its sparkle, feel its warmth, and receive illumination anew through its crystalline words.

There are five columns in this table:

1. The number. This column counts your treasures. If you find more *diamonds*, you may enter them after number 32. The numbers need not be sequential in relation to where the scriptures occur, although the first 32 are in order. These numbers are really the chronological sequence of when you collect your *diamonds*.

2. The reference. Because the context is already identified in the table header ("Doctrine and Covenants"), you need not enter "D&C" next to each reference.

3. The date. This is the date you collect your *diamond* (memorize and mark it). No explorer worth his salt would collect a treasure and not record the date of the discovery. The date is good for reference and an authentic history.

4. The key words. These help you remember the essence of the scripture, so that when you are looking for a *diamond* you can locate it quickly. What good are *diamonds* if you can't find them when you need them?

5. The association. Use this column to enter a key association or cross reference. For example, you might enter "Ruth's favorite" to associate a scripture to your sister Ruth and assist in remembering this scripture, in effect adding more brilliance to the *diamond*. You may also enter a cross reference to another scripture or to a journal entry. A journal cross reference is valuable. For example, by entering "J3-24," you know that in journal notebook 3, page 24, you have more information about this *diamond*. In this journal entry, then, you can record experiences, lessons, insights, history, and add more cross references. These cross references in your journal can be to other scriptures, to publications, to other journal entries where you develop your ideas further, and so on. In this way, the *diamond* table entry may become an index point to many more treasures. Refer to *Collecting journal entries and side-expeditions* on page 95.

Doctrine and Covenants - *Diamond* scriptures ◆				
#	Scripture	Date	Key Words	Association
1	1:31		sin - least degree of allowance	
2	3:2		crooked paths	
3	3:7		should not have feared man	
4	6:12		trifle not	
5	6:23		did I not speak peace to your mind	
6	6:36		every thought	
7	10:4		do not run faster	
8	18:10		worth of souls	
9	20:7		gave commandments	
10	25:12		song of the heart	
11	38:30		if ye are prepared	
12	42:14		Spirit, teach	
13	46:8		seek ye earnestly the best gifts	
14	50:23		not edify is not of God	
15	58:4		after much tribulation	
16	58:42		he who has repented of his sins	
17	81:5		succor the weak, lift up the hands	
18	82:10		I the Lord am bound	
19	84:36		he that receiveth my servants	
20	88:15		spirit, body, soul	

Doctrine and Covenants - *Diamond* scriptures ◆				
#	Scripture	Date	Key Words	Association
21	88:34		governed by law	
22	88:63		draw near unto me	
23	88:83		he that seeketh me early	
24	88:86		abide ye in the liberty	
25	88:124		cease to be idle	
26	93:36		glory, intelligence	
27	112:10		be thou humble	
28	130:18		intelligence will rise with us	
29	130:21		obtain any blessing is by obedience	
30	131:6		impossible to be saved in ignorance	
31	133:5		go ye out of Babylon	
32	137:9		judge according to works, desire	
33				
34				
35				
36				
37				
38				
39				
40				

Color-in graphics for diamond scriptures

The following two pages contain graphic letters that are to be colored red when each *diamond* is "collected"--that is, memorized and marked. See page 64, *How to collect diamond scriptures*. For example, when D&C 1:31 is collected, color the **T** of **TREASURES** on page 73 with a red marking pencil. When D&C 3:2 is collected, color the **R**, and so on through all the letters, so that when you color the last **E** of **KNOWLEDGE** you will have collected all the *diamonds* on page 73, signifying that you have memorized and marked each one in your scriptures.

You may use photocopies of these and other graphics in this guide to preserve the originals.

The graphic **TREASURES of KNOWLEDGE** is taken from D&C 89:19:

> And shall find wisdom and great <u>treasures of knowledge</u>, even hidden treasures.

The graphic **DRAW NEAR UNTO ME** is taken from D&C 88:63:

> <u>Draw near unto me</u> and I will draw near unto you; seek me diligently and ye shall find me: ask, and ye shall receive; knock, and it shall be opened unto you.

TREASURES

✦	T	D&C 1:31
✦	R	D&C 3:2
✦	E	D&C 3:7
✦	A	D&C 6:12
✦	S	D&C 6:23
✦	U	D&C 6:36
✦	R	D&C 10:4
✦	E	D&C 18:10
✦	S	D&C 20:7

OF

KNOWLEDGE

✦	K	D&C 25:12
✦	N	D&C 38:30
✦	O	D&C 42:14
✦	W	D&C 46:8
✦	L	D&C 50:23
✦	E	D&C 58:4
✦	D	D&C 58:42
✦	G	D&C 81:5
✦	E	D&C 82:10

DRAW

- ◆ D   D&C 84:36
- ◆ R   D&C 88:15
- ◆ A   D&C 88:34
- ◆ W   D&C 88:63

NEAR

- ◆ N   D&C 88:83
- ◆ E   D&C 88:86
- ◆ A   D&C 88:124
- ◆ R   D&C 93:36

UNTO

- ◆ U   D&C 112:10
- ◆ N   D&C 130:18
- ◆ T   D&C 130:21
- ◆ O   D&C 131:6

ME

- ◆ M   D&C 133:5
- ◆ E   D&C 137:9

Planting trees

Tree scriptures are larger than *diamond* verses, and require more work to bring home and plant. But they will sink their roots deep into the earth, become strong and beautiful, grow many branches, and provide fruit. And because they are "ever" green, they will give you shade from the heat of the sun, protect you from the wintry blast, and beautify the yard of your home and mansion in all seasons.

Trees are one of God's greatest creations. From them we make beautiful furniture, build homes, and carve tools and handiwork. Birds lodge in their branches. They have an aura about them, a mystic character. They inspire. They grow in many varieties, and all are marvels of beauty. What would life be without trees?

So too with the scriptures.

One of the best scriptures on trees is in the first Psalm. The person whose delight is in the law of the Lord (the scriptures), and frequently ponders and studies the teachings of God, will be:

> ... like a tree planted by the rivers of water, that bringeth
> forth his fruit in his season; his leaf also shall not wither;
> and whatsoever he doeth shall prosper.
> Psalms 1:3

Therefore, as this verse teaches, the scriptures will help **us** become trees. Planted by rivers of water. With fruit in season, leaves that do not wither, and whatsoever we do shall prosper. (See also D&C 97:9).

We will also become trees in the sense that by obtaining the word of the Lord, we can become living scriptures and impart their fruit and shade and beauty, nourished by living waters, all for the benefit of the weary traveler we may serve.

How to plant tree scriptures:

There are 29 *tree* scriptures you may plant in this expedition. These are identified in four places: the *tree* symbol (♣) in the Captain's Log (pp. 5-57), the boxed *tree* scriptures (pp. 77-81), the *tree* table (p. 83), and the color-in graphics (pp. 85-86).

You "plant" a *tree* scripture in the same way that you "collect" a *diamond* scripture: by memorizing and marking it. To assist in memorizing, *tree* scriptures are provided to photocopy and cut out on pages 77-81. Also see *Why memorize?* on page 94.

To mark a *tree* scripture:

1. Enter a green "∧" symbol (inverted v), resembling a tree, in the margin next to the scripture.

2. Highlight the scripture with a colored pencil, such as by underscoring or shading. This marking need not be in green, since the *tree* symbol in the margin is in green. Because a *tree* may not include every word in a scripture, highlight only the words of the *tree*; that is, the words you will memorize. Refer to pages 77-81 to see the suggested words for each *tree*.

3. Enter the scripture information in the *tree* table (p. 83) that you will insert into your scriptures. The scripture reference and key words for 29 *trees* are already entered in the table. All you have to do at this point is enter the date for the given scripture when you memorize and mark it. You may enter the association portion of the table later. This table is important because you can always refer to it to find your *trees*, and it will help in reviewing your memorizations.

After memorizing and marking a *tree* scripture, go to the color-in graphics on pages 85-86. Color (in green) the appropriate letter that matches the given scripture, to signify that you have planted this *tree* in the yard of your mansion, that you have transplanted and preserved it from your expedition into the Doctrine and Covenants.

🌲 *Tree* scriptures:

Seek not for riches but for wisdom, and behold, the mysteries of God shall be unfolded unto you, and then shall you be made rich. Behold, he that hath eternal life is rich.

D&C 6:7 🌲

Seek not to declare my word, but first seek to obtain my word, and then shall your tongue be loosed; then, if you desire, you shall have my Spirit and my word, yea, the power of God unto the convincing of men."

D&C 11:21 🌲

Yea, behold, I will tell you in your mind and in your heart, by the Holy Ghost, which shall come upon you and which shall dwell in your heart.

D&C 8:2 🌲

For behold, I, God, have suffered these things for all, that they might not suffer if they would repent; But if they would not repent they must suffer even as I."

D&C 19:16-17 🌲

You must study it out in your mind; then you must ask me if it be right, and if it is right I will cause that your bosom shall burn within you; therefore, you shall feel that it is right.

D&C 9:8 🌲

Wherefore, verily I say unto you that all things unto me are spiritual, and not at any time have I given unto you a law which was temporal.

D&C 29:34 🌲

Ye are not sent forth to be taught, but to teach the children of men the things which I have put into your hands by the power of my Spirit.

D&C 43:15 🌲

Wherefore, be not weary in well-doing, for ye are laying the foundation of a great work. And out of small things proceedeth that which is great.

D&C 64:33 🌲

For behold, it is not meet that I should command in all things; for he that is compelled in all things, the same is a slothful and not a wise servant; wherefore he receiveth no reward.

D&C 58:26 🌲

Behold, the Lord requireth the heart and a willing mind; and the willing and obedient shall eat the good of the land of Zion in these last days.

D&C 64:34 🌲

Verily I say, men should be anxiously engaged in a good cause, and do many things of their own free will, and bring to pass much righteousness.

D&C 58:27 🌲

And now ... this is the testimony, last of all, which we give of him: that he lives! For we saw him, even on the right hand of God: and we heard the voice bearing record that he is the Only Begotten of the Father.

D&C 76:22-23 🌲

For of him unto whom much is given much is required; and he who sins against the greater light shall receive the greater condemnation.

D&C 82:3 🌲

For what doth it profit a man if a gift is bestowed upon him, and he receive not the gift? Behold, he rejoices not in that which is given unto him, neither rejoices in him who is the giver of the gift.

D&C 88:33 🌲

And your minds in times past have been darkened because of unbelief, and because you have treated lightly the things you have received.

D&C 84:54 🌲

Teach ye diligently and my grace shall attend you, that you may be instructed more perfectly in theory, in principle, in doctrine, in the law of the gospel, in all things that pertain unto the kingdom of God, that are expedient for you to understand.   D&C 88:78 🌲

Neither take ye thought beforehand what ye shall say; but treasure up in your minds continually the words of life, and it shall be given you in the very hour that portion that shall be meted unto every man.

D&C 84:85 🌲

And as all have not faith, seek ye diligently and teach one another words of wisdom; yea, seek ye out of the best books words of wisdom; seek learning, even by study and also by faith.

D&C 88:118 🌲

Organize yourselves; prepare every needful thing; and establish a house, even a house of prayer, a house of fasting, a house of faith, a house of learning, a house of glory, a house of order, a house of God.

D&C 88:119 ♣

All truth is independent in that sphere in which God has placed it, to act for itself, as all intelligence also; otherwise there is no existence.

D&C 93:30 ♣

All saints who remember to keep and do these sayings ... shall find wisdom and great treasures of knowledge, even hidden treasures; And shall run and not be weary, and shall walk and not faint.

D&C 89:18-20 ♣

For I, the Lord, will cause them to bring forth as a very fruitful tree which is planted in a goodly land, by a pure stream, that yieldeth much precious fruit.

D&C 97:9 ♣

Search diligently, pray always, and be believing, and all things shall work together for your good, if ye walk uprightly and remember the covenant wherewith ye have covenanted one with another.

D&C 90:24 ♣

Wherefore, now let every man learn his duty, and to act in the office in which he is appointed, in all diligence. He that is slothful shall not be counted worthy to stand.

D&C 107:99-100 ♣

Therefore, strengthen your brethren in all your conversation, in all your prayers, in all your exhortations, and in all your doings.

D&C 108:7   ♣

Brethren, shall we not go on in so great a cause? Go forward and not backward. Courage, brethren; and on, on to the victory!

D&C 128:22   ♣

No power or influence can or ought to be maintained by virtue of the priesthood, only by persuasion, by long-suffering, by gentleness and meekness, and by love unfeigned.

D&C 121:41   ♣

We believe that governments were instituted of God for the benefit of man; and that he holds men accountable for their acts in relation to them.

D&C 134:1   ♣

Let thy bowels also be full of charity towards all men, and to the household of faith, and let virtue garnish thy thoughts unceasingly; then shall thy confidence wax strong in the presence of God.

D&C 121:45   ♣

The tree table:

Like the *diamond* table, you may photocopy the *tree* table (p. 83), cut out the table, fold at the middle, and insert inside the front or back cover of your scriptures.

This table is, first, the train car into which you put your *tree* seedlings so you can bring them home from your expedition; second, it becomes the yard of your mansion into which you plant your *trees* and nourish them as they grow and become fruitful. You can then go into your yard when you want to enjoy your *trees*, pick some fruit, receive of their shade, and so on.

There are five columns in this table:

1. The number. This column counts your *trees*. Your *trees* are numbered and you will know each one, as God knows each of his children. You will begin with 29 *trees*. If you want to plant other *trees*, you may enter them after number 29.

2. The reference. Because the context is already identified in the table header ("Doctrine and Covenants"), you need not enter "D&C" next to each reference.

3. The date. This is the date you plant your *tree* (memorize and mark it).

4. The key words. These help you remember the essence of the scripture, so that when you are looking for a *tree* you can find it.

5. The association. Use this column to enter a key association or cross reference. See explanation for the *diamond* table on page 70.

Doctrine and Covenants - *Tree scriptures* 🌲				
#	Scripture	Date	Key Words	Association
1	6:7		seek not for riches	
2	8:2		mind, heart, Holy Ghost	
3	9:8		study it out in your mind	
4	11:21		first seek to obtain my word	
5	19:16-17		God, suffered these things for all	
6	29:34		all things spiritual	
7	43:15		not sent to be taught	
8	58:26		not meet, command in all things	
9	58:27		anxiously engaged in a good cause	
10	64:33		be not weary, out of small things	
11	64:34		heart, willing mind	
12	76:22-23		testimony, last of all	
13	82:3		unto whom much is given	
14	84:54		minds darkened because of unbelief	
15	84:85		treasure up in your minds continually	
16	88:33		if receive not the gift	
17	88:78		teach ye diligently	
18	88:118		seek ye out of the best books	
19	88:119		organize yourselves	
20	89:18-20		shall find wisdom and great treasures	

Doctrine and Covenants - *Tree scriptures* 🌲				
#	Scripture	Date	Key Words	Association
21	90:24		all things shall work ... for your good	
22	93:30		all truth is independent	
23	97:9		as a very fruitful tree	
24	107:99-100		let every man learn his duty	
25	108:7		strengthen your brethren	
26	121:41		only by persuasion	
27	121:45		let virtue garnish thy thoughts	
28	128:22		go forward and not backward	
29	134:1		governments instituted of God	
30				
31				
32				
33				
34				
35				
36				
37				
38				
39				
40				

Color-in graphics for tree scriptures

The following two pages contain graphic letters that are to be colored green when each *tree* is planted--that is, memorized and marked. See page 75, *How to plant tree scriptures*. For example, when D&C 6:7 is planted, color the **o** of **OUT** on page 85 with a green marking pencil. Color the **U** of **OUT** when D&C 8:2 is planted, and so on through all the letters.

The graphic **OUT OF SMALL THINGS** is taken from D&C 64:33:

> Wherefore, be not weary in well-doing, for ye
> are laying the foundation of a great work.
> And <u>out of small things</u> proceedeth that which
> is great.

The graphic **A FRUITFUL TREE** is taken from D&C 97:9:

> For I, the Lord, will cause them to bring forth
> as <u>a</u> very <u>fruitful tree</u> which is planted in a
> goodly land, by a pure stream, that yieldeth
> much precious fruit.

OUT OF

🌲   O   D&C 6:7
🌲   U   D&C 8:2
🌲   T   D&C 9:8

🌲   O   D&C 11:21
🌲   F   D&C 19:16-17

SMALL

🌲   S   D&C 29:34
🌲   M   D&C 43:15
🌲   A   D&C 58:26
🌲   L   D&C 58:27
🌲   L   D&C 64:33

THINGS

🌲   T   D&C 64:34
🌲   H   D&C 76:22-23
🌲   I   D&C 82:3
🌲   N   D&C 84:54
🌲   G   D&C 84:85
🌲   S   D&C 88:33

A

🌲 A   D&C 88:78

FRUITFUL

🌲	F	D&C 88:118
🌲	R	D&C 88:119
🌲	U	D&C 89:18-20
🌲	I	D&C 90:24
🌲	T	D&C 93:30
🌲	F	D&C 97:9
🌲	U	D&C 107:99-100
🌲	L	D&C 108:7

TREE

🌲	T	D&C 121:41
🌲	R	D&C 121:45
🌲	E	D&C 128:22
🌲	E	D&C 134:1

Collecting mountain stones

Mountain *stones* are not individual scriptures, but summaries of the more important sections of the Doctrine and Covenants. After you excavate an important section, bringing out *diamonds*, *trees*, and other treasures, you will want a *stone* to signify the mountain from which you extracted your wealth, and to remember its snow-covered peaks and beautiful valleys. The Δ symbol marks the more significant or first tier of *mountain* sections, and the ▲ symbol marks the second tier of mountain sections. These are mountain *stones*, symbols you enter with a blue pencil at the beginning of chosen sections that have the tallest and most important peaks.

How to collect mountain stones:

There are 14 large mountain *stones* and 30 small mountain *stones* you may collect in this expedition. These are identified in two places: (1) the large mountain symbol (Δ) and the small mountain symbol (▲) in the Captain's Log at the beginning of a given section; and (2) the color-in graphics on pages 89-91. These designations are of course arbitrary, but will help in your study. Some of these sections are small in physical size, but marked as mountains to signify their importance.

You "collect" a mountain *stone* by first memorizing a section summary. The section summaries are provided in the graphics on pages 89-91. Second, you mark the section in your scriptures as a *mountain*.

To mark a section as a *mountain*:

- Enter a mountain symbol at the section heading in your scriptures. Use a blue colored pencil to draw the symbol. Mountains often have a blue appearance from a distance, and a blue sky frames them. Differentiate the larger mountains, the Δ from the ▲ symbols, by simply drawing a larger mountain symbol; or, alternatively, enter two Δ's side by side (ΔΔ) for your larger mountains. Enter the given symbol prominently next to the section number in your scriptures, so your eye will easily detect that this section is a *mountain*.

- Highlight in blue the summary words that you memorize. These words are often found in the section heading. For example, in Section 1 highlight *the Lord's Preface* in the last sentence of the section heading. If the section heading does not contain sufficient summary words, look in the verse summaries below the section heading. For example, in Section 93 highlight the words *truth* and *intelligence* in the verse summaries. Finally, look in a prominent scripture in the section. For example, in Section 9 highlight *to Oliver Cowdery* in the section heading, then highlight *study it out in your mind* in verse 8. In the latter case, a blue colored box around these words will usually not conflict with other markings you might have on verse 8.

Color-in graphics for mountain stones

The following three pages contain graphic letters that are to be colored blue when the appropriate section summary is collected--that is, memorized and marked. See page 87, *How to collect mountain stones.* For example, when you memorize the summary for D&C Section 1, which is *The Lord's Preface,* and have marked the heading of Section 1, color the **T** of **THE** on page 89 with a blue marking pencil. The summary for each section, that you are to memorize, is provided in the graphic.

Before you color the next letter, you must pass off all the previous letters again. For example, when you have colored all three letters of **THE**, you will be able to recite that Section 1 is *The Lord's Preface,* that Section 20 is on *Church organization and government,* and that Section 25 is *To Emma Smith - the song of the righteous.* And so on through all the letters of this graphic, so that when you color the last **E** of **LIFE** on page 89 you can recite the summaries of all the sections of this graphic. Follow this same pattern for the graphics on pages 90 and 91. Each graphic is a unit, so that all the words colored blue in one graphic will signify you can recite in sequence all the section summaries of that graphic. And because you are also marking these in your scriptures, you will have marked each of these section headings with a mountain symbol and highlighted the section summaries in blue.

The graphic **THE WORDS OF LIFE** is for large *mountains* (Δ symbol), and represents the first tier of section summaries worth knowing. It is taken from D&C 84:85:

> Neither take ye thought beforehand what ye
> shall say, but treasure up in your minds
> continually the words of life, and it shall be
> given you in the very hour that portion that
> shall be meted unto every man.

The second two graphics, **ORGANIZE YOURSELVES** and **HOUSE OF ORDER**, are for small *mountains* (▲ symbol), and represent the second tier of section summaries worth knowing. These are taken from D&C 88:119:

> Organize yourselves; prepare every needful
> thing; and establish a house, even a house of
> prayer, a house of fasting, a house of faith, a
> house of learning, a house of glory, a house
> of order, a house of God.

THE

Δ	T	D&C 1	The Lord's Preface
Δ	H	D&C 20	Church organization and government
Δ	E	D&C 25	To Emma Smith - the song of the righteous

WORDS

Δ	W	D&C 42	The law of the Church
Δ	O	D&C 76	Vision of the degrees of glory
Δ	R	D&C 84	Revelation on priesthood
Δ	D	D&C 88	The olive leaf
Δ	S	D&C 89	The Word of Wisdom

OF LIFE

Δ	O	D&C 93	Truth and intelligence
Δ	F	D&C 121	Prayer and prophecies from Liberty Jail
Δ	L	D&C 132	The marriage covenant
Δ	I	D&C 133	The appendix - Second Coming
Δ	F	D&C 134	Governments and laws in general
Δ	E	D&C 138	The Savior's visit to the spirits in prison

ORGANIZE

▲	O	D&C 3	Relating to the loss of 116 pages
▲	R	D&C 4	To Joseph Smith Sr. - ye that embark in the service of God
▲	G	D&C 5	To Martin Harris - three witnesses shall testify
▲	A	D&C 6	To Oliver Cowdery - exercise thy gift!
▲	N	D&C 7	Translated record of John
▲	I	D&C 8	To Oliver Cowdery - the spirit of revelation
▲	Z	D&C 9	To Oliver Cowdery - study it out in your mind
▲	E	D&C 10	Relating to the loss of 116 pages (cont. from section 3)

YOUR-

▲	Y	D&C 11	To Hyrum Smith - first seek to obtain my word
▲	O	D&C 19	God has suffered for all
▲	U	D&C 29	Signs, Second Coming, final judgment, atonement
▲	R	D&C 45	Signs, Second Coming, Millennium, New Jerusalem

SELVES

▲	S	D&C 46	Gifts of the Spirit
▲	E	D&C 50	Manifestations of different spirits
▲	L	D&C 58	Jackson Co., Missouri - anxiously engaged
▲	V	D&C 59	The Sabbath
▲	E	D&C 77	An explanation of the Revelation of St. John
▲	S	D&C 87	Revelation and prophecy on war

Establish a:

HOUSE

▲ H D&C 107 Melchizedek and Aaronic Priesthood
▲ O D&C 109 Dedication of the Kirtland Temple
▲ U D&C 110 Moses, Elias, and Elijah commit their keys
▲ S D&C 122 From Liberty Jail
▲ E D&C 123 From Liberty Jail

OF

▲ O D&C 128 Directions on baptism for the dead
▲ F D&C 129 Keys to distinguish angels

ORDER

▲ O D&C 130 Celestial earth, intelligence, law, Father has a body
▲ R D&C 131 The celestial glory, all spirit is matter
▲ D D&C 135 By John Taylor - martyrdom of Joseph Smith
▲ E D&C 136 By Brigham Young - organize for the westward journey
▲ R D&C 137 The Prophet sees his brother Alvin in the celestial kingdom

Collecting hidden treasures

Hidden treasures are not identified in any map here. But there are many *hidden treasures* to be found. The Lord has promised, "If thou wilt inquire, thou shalt know mysteries which are great and marvelous; therefore thou shalt exercise thy gift." (D&C 6:11)   As you study the scriptures and inquire, the Lord will enlighten your mind (D&C 6:15), and if you first seek to obtain his word, and deny not the spirit of revelation (D&C 11:21, 25), the Spirit will guide you to hidden groves, to valleys of peace, trails of wisdom, and "great treasures of knowledge, even hidden treasures" (D&C 89:19). Cherish these. Pack them away in your luxury car. Tag them and identify them with markings, even hidden markings. In this you will run and not be weary, walk and not faint, and the destroying angel will pass you by.

<u>*How to collect hidden treasures:*</u>

In this expedition there are two kinds of *hidden treasures*:

- A scripture that impresses you deeply enough that you want to catalogue it, and probably memorize it, apart from the *diamond* and *tree* scriptures. To collect this *hidden treasure*, refer to *Personal scripture table* below.

- Inspirations, thoughts, and ideas not associated with just one scripture in a table. To collect these *hidden treasures*, refer to *Collecting journal entries and side-expeditions* on page 95.

<u>*Personal scripture table*</u>:

For *hidden treasure* scriptures you want to collect apart from the *diamond* and *tree* scriptures already identified, you may use the blank table provided on page 93. Copy, cut, and insert into your scriptures. Follow the pattern on page 70 for making entries in this table. Unlike the *diamond* and *tree* tables, the entries in this table are not pre-determined. This table is for treasures you collect on your own.

You may use this table for any set of scriptures, not just the Doctrine and Covenants. For a given table, you should enter a unique table heading; for example, if you collect several scriptures from the Book of Psalms, you may dedicate one table solely to Psalms, by writing "Psalms" in the table heading, then by numbering and entering the scriptures from Psalms in this table.

#	Scripture	Date	Key Words	Association																			

#	Scripture	Date	Key Words	Association																			

Why memorize?

A key part of this expedition is memorization. People ask me, "Can I go on your expedition without memorizing?" Yes, you can. For example, you may simply complete the Captain's Log. That is a good expedition by itself. But if you want more treasures, they will be commensurate with your effort. Don't sell yourself short. Collect the treasures! Plant the trees!

In the introduction, I indicated there would be some coal to shovel. The coal is needed for heat and energy to fuel the engine of your expedition. Memorizing is like shoveling coal. It can be hard. But you develop muscles. You feel good. An unseen energy is released from the coal when it reaches combustion temperature. This energy fires your soul. Inspiration flows. In memorizing you will feel this energy, and through this power you will see new light in your *diamonds*, and your *trees* will grow and bear fruit.

What else can memorizing be likened to? Memorizing is like a song--you sing it with your heart and energize it with the timber of your faith. Memorizing is like collecting acorns--you save them in the storehouse of your mind, for use in time of need, and to settle into the soil of your subconscious to sprout into miraculous trees. Memorizing is like a talent--you develop it, master its secrets, and use your skill in all your travels. Memorizing is like a shield on your thoughts and attitudes--by which you can "keep *and* guard your heart with all vigilance, for out of it flow the springs of life" (Proverbs 4:23, *Amplified Bible*). Memorizing is like the Word of Wisdom--"a principle with promise, adapted to the capacity of the weak and the weakest of all saints" (D&C 89:3).

Who memorizes? Everyone memorizes, or has memorized, to one degree or another, including children, students, missionaries, professionals, great people like Winston Churchill, and Jesus. Yes, Jesus frequently recited scriptures in his mortal life. And if he did it, we should also do it. He said, "Follow me, and do the things which ye have seen me do" (2 Nephi 31:12). We will have power through him: "In me there is all power. Therefore, follow me, and listen to the counsel which I shall give unto you" (D&C 100:1-2). He encourages us to "treasure up in your minds continually the words of life" (D&C 84:85), and to "*exercise thy gift*, that thou mayest find out mysteries" (D&C 6:11).

How good do memorizations have to be? Well, this expedition is for **all** ages and personalities. So, there are allowances. Memorizing does not mean that you must recite a scripture and reference flawlessly and on demand. But it does mean that you review the selection carefully. You ponder. You think about each word and its place in the verse. Then you practice until you can recite the words from memory. Thereafter, you review as often as your love of that scripture impels you, according to your desires. Don't fret if you seem to forget a scripture over time, for it will always be there; and because in this expedition you highlight your memorizations, and enter them in tables, you can easily find them again. You will never lose them!

Collecting journal entries and side-expeditions

This final map is open-ended, and is to be used in conjunction with treasures you collect with the other maps. This map is an expedition journal, where you record many things not possible in the Captain's Log. This journal is simply a notebook. It need not be hard-bound or elegant. I recommend common spiral-bound notebooks containing about 70 or 80 pages. They are inexpensive, easy to carry and store, and designed for writing. On the front cover of the notebook, write the journal number and the date of your first entry, then later enter the end date here as well, which will be the date of the last entry, when the notebook is filled. Number each page in the notebook, so that when referencing your journals you can refer to journal number and page number.

Side-expeditions are little journeys you take on the spur of the moment as the Spirit directs. While you are on an expedition, and the train is stopped, you may see a valley or a trail you want to follow. The train will wait. Collect the treasures you find on these side-expeditions in your journal. When you are on any expedition into the scriptures, whether or not in the Doctrine and Covenants, you should record your discoveries, your inspirations, and your research. For example, when preparing a talk, giving a lesson, or pondering the scriptures, record your insights and thoughts in your journal. Draw a line across the page to separate from the last entry, record the current date, and then write. Do not worry about spelling and grammar, or if for a lesson or talk, about arranging everything in the right order. Just write what comes to you when it comes. You can reorganize later and enter into your computer or into a final format, for a separate collection of finalized notes and lessons. Note that although today's topic is scripture study, you can intersperse many kinds of entries in your journal.

Another facet of collecting hidden treasures in your scripture expeditions is scripture marking in general. You will want to mark many scriptures that you do not memorize or document in a table or journal as suggested in this book. Nevertheless, what is presented here should complement any marking strategy you already have. And if you are just beginning to mark your scriptures, you will have a good start by following the maps in this expedition, which guide you to mark memorized scriptures in a unique way (the *diamond* and *tree* symbols) and record them in the tables provided. From this simple beginning you will find that other markings will revolve around these. Your memorized scriptures will be "stakes" that hold up the tent of all your scripture markings.

But back to expedition journals. Following is an example of a side-expedition I recorded in my journal some time ago. I include it here because it answers the important question, *Where is the Urim and Thummim today?*

January 26, 1980

On revelation through scripture study --

While preparing a lesson from the Book of Ether, I read where the brother of Jared went unto a mountain and received, in addition to the shining stones to light his people's ships, two additional stones (see Ether 3:1, 23, 28). These two stones were the Urim and Thummim. I soon became intrigued with this curious instrument. I pondered its history. I looked up other references in the scriptures, I read commentaries that gave additional insight . . .

From this beginning in my journal, I added upon and made notes from which I can now present the following:

Where is the Urim and Thummim today?

There are several references in the Old Testament to the Urim and Thummim: Exodus 28:30, Leviticus 8:8, Numbers 27:21, Deuteronomy 33:8, I Samuel 28:6, Ezra 2:63, and Nehemiah 7:65. From these we learn that Moses and Aaron had the instrument and transmitted it to their priesthood successors. From other scriptures we learn that Abraham had the Urim and Thummim, through which he saw the stars, the throne of God, and many marvelous visions (Abraham 3:1-4). The Brother of Jared had it (Ether 3:21-28). Mosiah also had it (Mosiah 8:13), and other Nephite prophets until Moroni deposited it with the Gold Plates (Ether 4:5, D&C 17:1). From there Joseph Smith received it and used it in the translation of the Book of Mormon (Joseph Smith History -- 1:35) and in receiving other revelations (see headings to D&C Sections 3, 6, 7, 11, 14, 17).

Do you think other prophets might have had the Urim and Thummim but did not tell us? The instrument is too sacred to be known to the world, and has been guarded closely by angels and prophets over the centuries.

The following comments of Dr. Sperry are especially interesting. Do you agree with his assertions about how the instrument might have worked in the revelation process?

> In all probability the active elements in the instrument, that is to say, the two stones, were composed of celestial material. That the stones of the Urim and Thummim were from the celestial world [is] a fact of supreme importance--in any attempted explanation of how they functioned. Somehow or other, celestial material seems to have helped both ancient and modern seers to bridge the chasm of the unknown.
>
> ... the celestial stones of the Urim and Thummim enabled the Seer, by concentrating all of his spiritual faculties, to pass into the realm of the unknown and have the truth made known to him. Using a technical term familiar to the chemist, the Urim and Thummim were in effect spiritual "catalyzers"--they promoted an action that otherwise would not readily go forward without their use.
>
> (Answers to Book of Mormon Questions, Sidney B. Sperry, Bookcraft, 1967, p. 18-19).

In I Samuel 28:6 of the Jerusalem Bible (a modern translation from ancient texts), the word "Urim" is translated as "oracle." Under the word "oracle" in the dictionary, the first definition is: "The medium by which a god reveals hidden knowledge or makes known the divine purpose." And the third definition is: "The revelation received from such a place or medium: the scriptures." There it is. The scriptures are an oracle, a kind of Urim and Thummim! Think about it. Review Dr. Sperry's explanation above and see if it does not apply also to the scriptures. Can you not think of the scriptures as celestial material that enhances your spiritual capacities, allowing you to pass into the realm where truth and revelation can more easily flow into your being?

Have you ever wished to have a look at the Urim and Thummim, and to gaze through those curious stones? Wouldn't it be a blessing to be worthy of such an honor? Wouldn't you, if given the chance, handle the instrument and think of the brother of Jared, of Abraham, Moses, Moroni, Joseph Smith, and others who had held and used those very stones? And most of all, wouldn't you want to receive some revelation through them while you were at it? You probably wouldn't ask for just any revelation either; but foremost in your mind would be revelation about yourself, your destiny, your talents, your family, and your life.

Well, you **can** do that, because you have a Urim and Thummim. Peer into the celestial material of the scriptures, and they will help you bridge the chasms of the unknown; and, if you concentrate your spiritual faculties, you will have truths made known to you. Through this Urim and Thummim God will reveal hidden knowledge and make known his divine purpose. The scriptures should command the same respect and reverence as the original Urim and Thummim. The scriptures have been handed down from Adam and the great prophets of ages gone by, "touched" by them as they reveal God's word through them. And now you too can handle them, peer into them, and receive great revelations about yourself, your life, your destiny, and your concerns.

This side-expedition example regarding the Urim and Thummim concludes the final map of this expedition. And this map, a humble journal, is in many ways the greatest map. In it, record your thoughts, inspirations, and side-expeditions, and you will become a master guide to lead and serve others.

So, in conclusion . . .

Good luck in your expedition through the Doctrine and Covenants. Collect the diamonds; through their crystalline faces you will have a Urim and Thummim. Plant the trees; they will embellish your mansion throughout this life and forever. Take side-expeditions and collect hidden treasures; they will add abundant wealth to your life.

PRD

Answers to questions in the Captain's Log:

1. Preface. 1: heading
2. Escape. 1:2
3. Disciples. 1:4
4. Recompense. Measure. 1:10
5. Commandments. 1:17
6. Weak. 1:19
7. Language. 1:24
8. Humble. 1:28
9. Sin. 1:31
10. Light. 1:33
11. Search. 1:37
12. No, no, yes. 1:38
13. The angel Moroni. 2: heading
14. Priesthood. 2:1
15. Promises. 2:2
16. Lehi. 3: heading
17. No. 3:1
18. Crooked. 3:2
19. Feared. 3:7
20. Gift. 3:11
21. Director. 3:15
22. His father, Joseph Smith, Sen. 4: heading
23. Heart, might, mind, strength. 4:2
24. Faith, hope, charity, love. 4:5
25. Martin Harris. 5: heading
26. My, all. 5:7
27. Three. 5:11
28. Heaven. 5:12
29. Power. 5:13
30. Moon, sun, army. 5:14
31. Yes. 5:24
32. Stand still. 5:34
33. Oliver Cowdery. 6: heading
34. Quick, powerful. 6:2
35. Wisdom, eternal life. 6:7
36 Desire, desire. 6:8
37. Gift, gift. 6:10
38. Trifle. 6:12
39. Enlighten, enlightened. 6:15
40. No. 6:16
41. Peace. 6:23
42. Good. 6:33
43. Look. 6:36
44. John. 7: heading
45. Death. 7:2
46. Kingdom. 7:4
47. Flaming, ministering. 7:6
48. Translation. 8: heading
49. Mind, heart. 8:2
50. Faith. 8:10
51. Translate. 9: heading
52. Thought, ask. 9:7
53. Mind, feel. 9:8
54. Stupor. 9:9
55. Three. See dates in headings of sections 3 and 10.
56. Darkened. 10:2
57. Strength, means. 10:4
58. Deeds, evil. 10:21
59. Deceive, deceive. 10:28
60. Gospel. 10:45
61. Contention, contention. 10:63
62. His brother, Hyrum Smith. 11: heading
63. Desireth. 11:3
64. Gift, gift. 11:10
65. Mind, soul. 11:13
66. Obtain, Spirit, word. 11:21
67. Revelation, Prophecy. 11:25
68. All. 11:27
69. Joseph Knight, Sen. 12: heading
70. Temperate. 12:8
71. John the Baptist. 13: heading
72. Messiah, ministering, repentance, remission. 13:1
73. Peter Whitmer, Sen. 14: heading
74. Eternal life. 14:7
75. Eight. 15: heading
76. Repentance. 15:6
77. Peter Whitmer, Jun. 16: heading
78. Yes. 16:4
79. Three. 17: heading
80. Plates, breastplate, sword, Urim and Thummim, directors. 17:1
81. Yes. 17:7
82. Melchizedek. 18: heading
83. Souls. 18:10
84. One soul. 18:15
85. Soberness. 18:21
86. Desires. 18:38
87. Eternal. 19: heading
88. Yes. 19:3
89. Endless, endless, Endless. 19:10
90. Suffer. 19:16
91. Glad, high. 19:29
92. Tenets. 19:31
93. Government. 20: heading
94. Commandments. 20:7
95. Grace. 20:30
96. Yes. 20:37
97. The elders. 20:45
98. Authority. 20:73
99. D&C 27:2-4, from footnote 79a
100. Church. 21: heading
101. April 6, 1830 21:3
102. Disperse, shake. 21:6
103. Rebaptism. 22: heading
104. Counsel. 22:4
105. Duties. 23: heading
106. Strengthen. 23:3
107. Encourage. 24: heading

223. Destroyer. 61: heading
224. Swiftly. 61:3
225. John. 61:14
226. One, all. 61:36
227. Weakness, succor. 62:1
228. Recorded, rejoice. 62:3
229. Judgment, directions. 62:8
230. Signs, wonders. 63:12
231. Mysteries, living. 63:23
232. Old, new. 63:49
233. Yes. 63:51
234. Sacred, constraint. 63:64
235. Hearts, afflicted. 64:8
236. Required, all. 64:10
237. Sacrifice, burned. 64:23
238. Weary, small. 64:33
239. Heart, willing. 64:34
240. Wonderful. 65:4
241. God. 65:5
242. Heaven. 65:6
243. Cumbered. 66:10
244. Magnify, everlasting. 66:11
245. Fears, receive. 67:3
246. Above, lights. 67:9
247. Quickened. 67:11
248. Minds, back. 67:14
249. Scripture, will, mind, word, voice. 68:4
250. Designated, worthy. 68:20
251. Parents. 68:25
252. Idlers, earnestly. 68:31
253. Knowledge. 69:7
254. Stewards. 70:3
255. Prepare, commandments, revelations. 71:4
256. Time, eternity. 72:3
257. Wise, time. 72:4
258. Bishop. 72:9
259. Missions. 73:2
260. 1 Corinthians 7:14. 74: heading
261. Holy. 74:7
262. Sheaves, honor. 75:5
263. Expedient. 75:10
264. Overcome. 75:16
265. John 5:29. 76: heading
266. Spirit, power. 76:10
267. Conversed. 76:14
268. He lives. 76:22
269. Yes. 76:28
270. Ordained. 76:48
271. Celestial. 76:70
272. Blinded. 76:75
273. Valiant. 76:79
274. No. 76:83
275. Yes. 76:98
276. Glory, might, dominion. 76:114
277. Revelation. 77: heading
278. Yes. 77:1
279. Light, knowledge, power. 77:4
280. Temporal. 77:6

281. Seventh. 77:13
282. Salvation. 78:16
283. Wise. 78:22
284. Glad, fear. 79:4
285. Believe, know. 80:4
286. Lift up, strengthen. 81:5
287. Given, required. 82:3
288. Former. 82:7
289. Bound, promise. 82:10
290. Beauty, holiness, arise. 82:14
291. Widows, orphans. 83:6
292. Priesthood. 84: heading
293. Melchizedek. 84:14
294. Priesthood. 84:17
295. Ordinances. 84:20
296. Ministering, preparatory. 84:26
297. Eight days old. 84:28
298. Sanctified, renewing. 84:33
299. Servants. 84:36
300. Truth, truth. 84:45
301. Unbelief. 84:54
302. Boast. 84:73
303. Friends, friends, friends. 84:77
304. Weary, darkened. 84:80
305. Treasure, continually. 84:85
306. Peace. 84:102
307. Remembrance. 85:9
308. Angels. 86:5
309. Savior. 86:11
310. War. 87: heading
311. South Carolina. 87:1
312. Stand, moved 87:8
313. Olive leaf. 88: heading
314. Enlighteneth. 88:11
315. Spirit, body. 88:15
316. Law. 88:22
317. Yes. 88:26
318. Receive. 88:33
319. Law, law. 88:34
320. Kingdoms. 88:47
321. Near, near, diligently. 88:63
322. Time, way, will. 88:68
323. Theory, principle, doctrine, law. 88:78
324. Heaven, earth. 88:79
325. Early. 88:83
326. Entangle. 88:86
327. Sign. 88:93
328. Silence. 88:95
329. Books, study, faith. 88:118
330. Organize, learning, order. 88:119
331. Idle, unclean, sleep. 88:124
332. Charity. 88:125
333. Word of Wisdom. 89: heading
334. Promise. 89:3
335. Strong drinks. 89:7
336. Tobacco. 89:8
337. Herbs. 89:10
338. Sparingly. 89:12

About the Author

Paul R. Day holds bachelor's and master's degrees in Computer and Information Science. He is employed by IBM as a computer systems designer.

Paul especially enjoys teaching gospel subjects. "I develop object lessons for my teaching," he explains, "then write them up on my personal computer for later use and to share with other teachers. I target these to be fun and instructive to all age groups." He is currently a stake missionary and visits a federal prison every other week where he teaches LDS inmates and investigators. "There are many good people in prison, and they need our love and help," he affirms. He also enjoys games, sports, reading, and writing. Doctrine and Covenants Expedition is his second published book, following Book of Mormon Expedition published in 1995.

Paul and his wife, Janice, live in Rochester, Minnesota, where they serve as stake missionaries. They have nine children and three grandchildren.

Acknowledgment

Artwork was contributed by Scott P. Day, oldest son of Paul and Janice.